A Step-by-Step Guide to Realizing Your Best

The family roi Experience

Barbara Fagan-Smith and Lesli Gee

Illustrations of Family ROI Journey Map and Family ROI Tree by Janet Schatzman & Associates, LLC

Design by Eric Bemberess

Family ROI, Family ROI Experience, Family ROI Tree, Family ROI Kids' Camp, Family ROI Journey Map, Family ROI Talking Stick and associated logos are trademarks of Family ROI.

Printed in the United States of America
First printing, December 2010

Published by Family ROI
5274 Scotts Valley Dr., Suite 207
Scotts Valley, CA 95066
www.familyroi.org

Library of Congress Control Number: 2010916454
ISBN 978-1456320164

Permissions

Grateful acknowledgment is made to the following for permission to reprint previously published material:

The material on page 51 and 81 is reprinted with permission from Running Press, a member of the Perseus Books Group, *The Book of New Family Traditions* by Meg Cox.

The story on page 149 is reprinted with permission from the October 1991 *Reader's Digest*; based on the original article, *Good Night Sister. Thank You for Teaching Me!* in *Proteus: A Journal of Ideas*, Spring 1991.

ACKNOWLEDGMENTS

We would like to express our deepest gratitude to those who helped us create and deliver the Family ROI Experience over the years. It has been an extraordinary journey together. Thank you also to all the families who have gone through the Family ROI Experience and those whose stories are shared in this book. We especially thank and applaud Colin Smith, Lisa Stambaugh, Moira Simpson, Jean Morrison, Sheryl Lewis, Janet Schatzman, Sloane Mann, Michelle Turner, Ann Marsh, Laura Petersen, Tami Adachi, and Angie Lackey.

We feel privileged to partner with our New Zealand friends, Rajen Prasad and Paul Curry from the Families Commission, and Fiona Inkpen and Chris Procter-Abraham from the Children's Health Camps.

Of course, we are grateful to our parents who have loved, encouraged, and supported us unconditionally—we feel fortunate to have learned what family truly means from David and Pat Fagan and Al and Sharon Gee.

Most especially, we wish to thank our husbands, Colin and Stan, and our children, Emma, Marina, Ryan, Jordan, and Lauren, since family is what it's all about.

thank you!

We invite you to think of your Family ROI experience as a journey.

Here you'll find the Family ROI Journey Map that your family can use as you move through each step of the experience.

Just as you would use a game board, your family can follow the path and stop at each road sign to complete the corresponding activity in the book. Some families find it fun to use a small game piece to mark their movement on the map.

At the end of each activity, you'll be asked to capture your family's discussion or agreements by writing directly on the journey map in the designated space. You can order a large version of the map at www.familyroi.org or make an enlarged copy at your local print shop.

Regardless of the format you choose, make the map unique to your own family. Write your family name in the airplane banner at the top and attach a family photo in the upper left-hand corner.

At the end of the Family ROI Experience, you will have a completed map that will serve as a visual reminder of your unique journey as a family.

Family Photo

2
Values

2. Values:
A set of agreed upon principles, qualities and beliefs that guide our decisions and actions as a family

Communication

1
Communication

1. Communication:
Speaking with honesty, listening with empathy, connecting, sharing and making plans together

Start Here

A.

B.

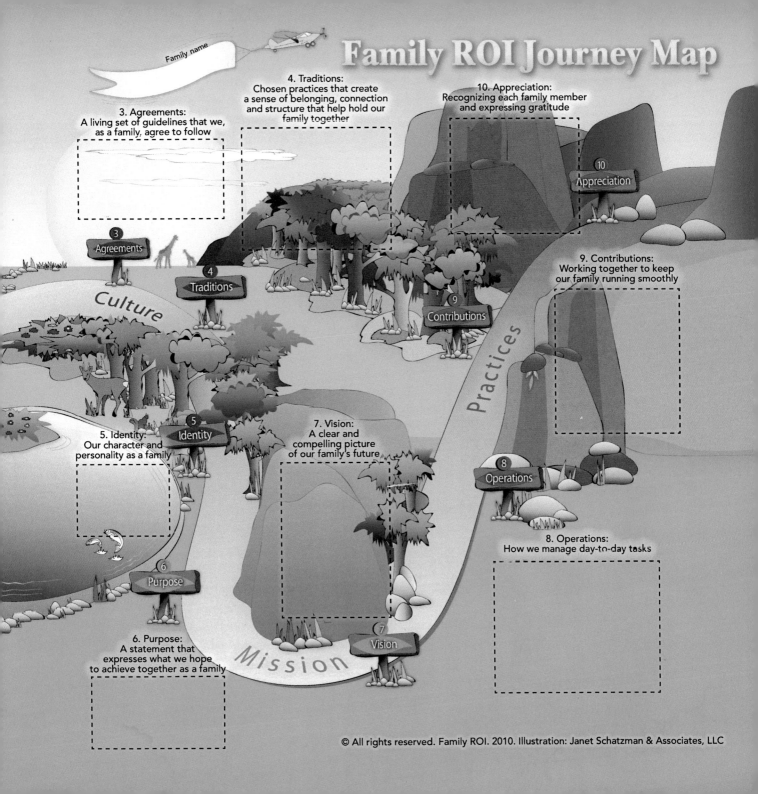

Family ROI Journey Map

Family name

3. Agreements:
A living set of guidelines that we, as a family, agree to follow

4. Traditions:
Chosen practices that create a sense of belonging, connection and structure that help hold our family together

10. Appreciation:
Recognizing each family member and expressing gratitude

9. Contributions:
Working together to keep our family running smoothly

5. Identity:
Our character and personality as a family

7. Vision:
A clear and compelling picture of our family's future

8. Operations:
How we manage day-to-day tasks

6. Purpose:
A statement that expresses what we hope to achieve together as a family

Culture

Practices

Mission

3 Agreements
4 Traditions
5 Identity
6 Purpose
7 Vision
8 Operations
9 Contributions
10 Appreciation

CONTENTS

BARBARA

The concept for Family ROI came to me in 1996, shortly after I experienced a crisis in my own marriage. At that time, my husband Colin and I were not getting along well, so I poured myself into the two areas of my life that were most rewarding: building my career and taking care of our one-year-old daughter, Emma. My daughter loved and needed me, and I loved her with all my heart and soul. My job was fun, and people there respected and admired me. My love for Colin lay buried where I couldn't feel it anymore under accumulated miscommunications and mutual frustration.

Fortunately, Colin and I found our way to a nonprofit organization called Retrouvaille that helps married couples in crisis.[1] The weekend retreat was a life-changing experience for both of us, and I was stunned by how close I had come to throwing away our partnership and the family we had created together. During that weekend and several follow-up Saturday sessions, we came to learn and internalize a deeper understanding of love and commitment. The experience brought us closer together than we had ever been before.

As we worked through our problems and grew stronger as a couple, I became aware of how I was putting most of my energy into my work and relatively little energy into the creative growth and development of our family. I also recognized how powerful certain time-tested principles and practices were at work, leading to tangible and sometimes spectacular professional results. Why not apply some of them to my family life? This was the start of Family ROI.

When you think about it, ideally, a family is an organization bound by love. Granted, it's not as large or as complex an organization as most businesses. But, I began to wonder,

- *Could certain business practices help my family function more cohesively and with a stronger sense of common purpose?*

- *Could they help us determine our vision for the future and give us a roadmap to achieve our most important goals?*

- *Could they help us identify and realize our most heartfelt values?*

- *Could they help us understand each other better and value each other even more?*

- *Could they save us time and energy, helping us eliminate some of the day-to-day pressures of our busy lives?*

By applying sound business principles, people have achieved extraordinary results in professional endeavors. We have sent astronauts to the moon and a Rover to Mars. We have built fuel-efficient cars and personal computers with wizard-like powers. We have found cures for diseases and created sublime works of art. I thought,

> *Why not apply some of these same, powerful practices to improve our lives at home, and to help each member in a family achieve his or her best, individually and collectively?*

With these questions in mind, I set about researching, brainstorming, and developing an approach to apply key business principles

to the family. Colin worked with me to test some of the techniques. Together, we began having strategic planning sessions. We developed a shared vision for our family and discussed how to achieve it. We talked about our most cherished values. We figured out ways to be more efficient and to relieve some of the everyday stresses of raising a family. Within months, we began to see amazing results. The work we did built a stronger foundation for our growing family. Soon we had our beautiful daughter Marina. We became much better equipped as parents and life partners to make the most of our good times and to weather the hard times.

> "By applying sound business principles, people have achieved extraordinary results in professional endeavors."

As the years go on, we continue to rely on these practices. They help in ways big and small, like improving the way our days began. Once both of our daughters were in school, we decided we needed to do something about our chaotic weekday mornings. In our household, there was no rhyme or reason to our morning routine. The girls didn't know what they wanted to wear to school. "Did you make the lunches?" I'd ask Colin, while encouraging Emma to decide between a dress or shorts. "I thought *you* made the lunches!" Colin replied. By the time we had all parted ways, everyone was feeling stressed and out of sorts. By identifying this as a problem area, we were able to step back and figure out how to structure our mornings. Now we work together smoothly as a team and our mornings are usually peaceful. Amazing!

We've used Family ROI to tackle much deeper challenges, too. After 25 years in the computer industry, Colin acknowledged, during one of our planning sessions, that he really didn't like his work. At the time, I was working part-time and Colin was working full-time. We realized we needed to swap roles. I went back to working full-time in a profession I love. Colin left the computer industry and began logging hours toward becoming certified as a flight instructor. Today, he teaches pilots how to fly single- and twin-engine planes, and he loves his work!

Now that Colin has achieved his dream of working in aviation, together our family has realized some of our most high-flying dreams. Colin has flown the four of us around the United States and Europe. He has also flown across the Atlantic, a long-held dream of his. We've also used the vision and planning tools in Family ROI to realize our

dream of living in other countries, including Spain and India. The girls attended school in both countries, and I continued to run the company I founded in California.

"We have experienced over and over that when our dreams are turned into clear visions, anything is possible!"

Back at home, a crumbling Victorian house we had always admired came onto the market four years ago. It was a home that we drove by frequently for more than ten years and dreamed of fixing it up. We ended up buying the home, and Colin led a team of workers to restore it to its glory. We have experienced over and over that when our dreams are turned into clear visions, anything is possible!

Now our girls, who are growing up quickly, join us in our annual visioning and strategic planning. They created our family logo and helped define our values and purpose as a family. They know firsthand the power of intention in creating the life you want to live.

Don't get me wrong; we still have our struggles. We have our bad days and weeks, as do all people and families. However, the relatively small investment of time and energy it takes to follow these practices continues to yield results. Emotionally, spiritually, materially, and in every other way, our family's Return on Investment (ROI) has been spectacular.

Over the years, Lesli and I, with our dynamic team at Family ROI, have had the privilege of helping hundreds of others apply these principles through the Family ROI Experience. I cherish the memory of spending time with my mother and father one weekend as they identified specific goals they wanted to realize during the years that remained to them. Being conscious of what they wanted, who they wanted to be with, and how they wanted to live helped make their last years better.

> Walt Disney said, "All our dreams can come true if we have the courage to pursue them."

Each of us has limited time on earth. The weeks and months and years of our lives speed by and our children grow up all too fast. That's why it's important to continually look for practical ways to make the most of our time, energy, and resources. Nowhere is this more important than at home, in our roles as parents and partners.

I hope the time you invest in Family ROI helps you come to know and understand your loved ones better, too, and that the things you learn make a positive difference in your lives for many years to come. Walt Disney said, "All our dreams can come true if we have the courage to pursue them." As you read *The Family ROI Experience,* I hope you will dream big dreams for yourself and your family. Using these practical skills and insights, you will be better equipped than ever to achieve them.

Warm regards,

Barbara

Barbara

LESLI

When people ask me what Family ROI is all about, I respond with a question of my own, "Are you living the life you want to be living?" Because that is what Family ROI is about: living with intention to design the life—and the family—that you dream of.

The seeds for Family ROI were planted in my heart all the way back in the second grade, in a classroom at St. Brigid's School in San Francisco, on the edge of Pacific Heights. That year, my classmate Kip Garney was diagnosed with leukemia.

A sweet, quiet boy, Kip missed school for just a few doctors' appointments at first. Then he started to be absent for longer periods of time. After he was hospitalized, we all wrote letters and drew silly cards to cheer him up.

His father came to visit our class and brought updates and stories about Kip. At age seven, it never even occurred to me that he might die, but one day the unthinkable happened.

Kip's death stunned me in a way nothing had up to that point in my life. At his funeral, all of us second graders formed a line on the church steps as the pallbearers passed in front of us. I will never forget the sight. *It's such a little casket,* I thought to myself. *Life is short.*

Kip's memory has stayed with me ever since then. I think of him whenever I hit a milestone in my life. *Kip never graduated from high school,* I thought. And later, *Kip never got to go to college. Kip never got married.* The experience filled me with a sense of responsibility to do all I can with whatever I have been given in my own life.

After graduating from UC Berkeley's School of Business, I went to work for Aetna Life and Casualty as an organization development specialist, leading strategic planning and visioning sessions for executives and their teams. I was excited to begin my career and to contribute. I was surrounded by people who invested heavily in their careers, regularly uprooted their families to relocate for promotions, and spent late hours in the office. This became my new normal. It was all I knew. Soon I was caught up in the same blur.

One night, a team of us stayed up all night, working intensely to finish plans for a large company reorganization. I was single, but many of my colleagues were married. I listened as they called home to check in and say good night to their kids. On the weekend, we were exhausted. That Saturday morning, it struck me that we were all devoting hours—and our best selves—perfecting strategic plans and PowerPoint decks, all to design an awesome experience for the company's employees. Yet none of us were putting a sliver of our best selves into designing awesome experiences for ourselves or our families. *Is this the way it's supposed to be?* I asked myself. *What if everyone put a fraction of the effort they invest in work into their families?* Thinking back to Kip, I wondered if I was

in the right place, spending my time on the right things, using my life as best as I could.

My boyfriend Stan (who eventually became my husband) and I pondered this question. We decided it might be fun to devote a weekend camping trip to talking about our future and doing some strategic planning— just for ourselves.

> "What if everyone put a fraction of the effort they invest in work into their families?"

We weren't sure how it would work out at first. But soon it became a fun and regular practice. During those few days in the woods, away from work and other distractions, we would dream of our goals for the coming year and for our life. Sometimes we kept it pretty simple—we jotted down handwritten lists on yellow legal pads, created collages with magazine pictures, or drew pictures with crayons. Other times, I brought along more formal visioning tools that I had used during the week with teams at work. We went through the same type of discussions— but for our personal life. The techniques themselves didn't matter as much as the fact that we fell into the habit of talking about our future and living with intention. We were amazed to find that the very act of declaring desires like "I want to do a triathlon," "I want to have a shorter commute," or "I want to get my master's degree" propelled us into action and magically made these intentions happen. These annual planning trips helped us prepare for marriage and eventually for parenthood, which soon grew to include our twin boys and daughter.

> "Gaining clarity about what you want and how to make it happen is a discipline, a habit, a muscle...."

Ten years later, I met Barbara while working at Quantum Corporation. We became friends and soon discovered that we both had been using strategic planning in our personal life and were both experiencing remarkable results. Our shared passion led to our collaboration on Family ROI.

Gaining clarity about what you want and how to make it happen is a discipline, a habit, a muscle—one that anyone can develop with some practice. By using the Family ROI tools, our family has been able to get clear on what matters most to us and achieve many dreams big and small, from Lauren learning how to ride her bike without training wheels to my running the Boston Marathon, to raising money for The Leukemia & Lymphoma Society. Right now we're on a mission to visit every Major League Baseball park in the United States (my kids' dream, not mine).

These are our dreams. Yours are surely different. You may dream of starting a garden in your backyard or sailing around the world or sending your child to college. You may dream of returning to college yourself. Whatever your dreams may be, you can realize them. We've seen the Family ROI tools work for families of all backgrounds.

> "Whatever your dreams may be, you can realize them."

For the record, I don't believe anyone has a perfect family. Neither Barbara nor I would make that claim for ourselves—far from it! Luckily, perfection is not what we're after here, just seeking the life we want to have, contributing to good, and finding happiness with the people we love.

When our twin boys were five, Stan and I attended their first Christmas pageant at school. I was inspired by the unrestrained passion and pride of the kindergarteners.

They sang with excitement, exuding joy with their whole beings, not caring at all what they looked like. The contrast with the more sullen, self-conscious junior high students was like day and night. I was struck with a thought that has stayed with me ever since, *What if each of these kids could grow up to truly reach their full potential?* The question lead naturally to others, including, *What if we all could become everything we hope and desire?* Sadly, many people do not reach their potential. Real life settles in, dreams are delayed or squashed. Hope and motivation dwindle. Soon they find themselves asking, "What happened?" "Where did it all go?," and "Can I still find a way to achieve my dreams?"

I believe with all my heart that the answer to the last question lies with the family. The family is the launching pad for every little person and for bigger ones, too. I also believe there is no blueprint for the perfect launching pad. It can be a single mom, a grandparent raising a grandchild, or a blended family. Regardless of their shape, if each family knew—really knew—how to propel each family member's bundle of gifts, energy, and passion towards good, imagine what our world would be like. Wow!

Asking these questions inspired me to help create Family ROI. I hope it helps you and your family live the life that you dream of.

Warm wishes,

Lesli

Lesli

INTRODUCTION

Realizing Your Best Family

Is your family as strong and successful as it can be? Are you living the life you've dreamed of?

After being barraged by the typical depressing news reports that we see each morning, we were pleasantly surprised to spot a refreshing headline the other day: For Happiness, Seek Family, Not Fortune: Study Shows Family Relationships Bring Greater Happiness Than High Income.

> "For Happiness, Seek Family, Not Fortune: Study Shows Family Relationships Bring Greater Happiness Than High Income."

Great news! A University of Texas at Austin study concluded that while money could buy happiness for some, strong family ties are a much bigger predictor of contentment than income for most people.[2]

This probably isn't surprising to most people. "Of course," we all say, nodding knowingly. "Family comes first. That's what's most important to *me*." Right?

Yet researcher Rebecca J. North says, "If you ask people about this, I think most would say that family relationships are more important than family income for happiness. But if you look at the way people allocate their time, you might get a different idea."

How about you? If a research study turned the microscope on your family, what would it see? Is your family as strong and successful as it could be? Is your family living the life you dream of? If so, wonderful!

Unfortunately, many families confide in us that they are not. They are beyond tired—they are exhausted. It's the morning carpool rush; the back-to-back meetings; the barrage of e-mails, texts, and tweets; the chauffeuring of overscheduled kids to triple-booked activities; the rush to pick up dinner; the struggles over homework...and then replaying the scene all over again the next morning.

But what if it could be different? What if you and your family could reset and live the life you imagine?

It is possible. We have found that families can become stronger by using some simple, proven practices that the most successful organizations around the globe use. At Family ROI, we've been helping people realize their best families by adopting these basic practices.

What does 'Family ROI' mean?

Family ROI is an organization dedicated to strengthening families by applying proven business practices to the family. For the past five years, we've been offering Family ROI Experiences, which are fun and engaging weekend retreats for people to revitalize, focus and strengthen their families.

Why ROI? ROI (Return on Investment) is a common financial term used in the business world to describe how well an investment delivers results. Every organization has to make choices about where to invest its money and resources. The most successful ones know

that to reach their goals, they need to create a solid business plan based on wise choices and investments. To make the best decision, they look at whether an investment will produce the greatest return for them.

In the same way, families also invest their time, energy, and love—sometimes deliberately, with intention, but many times quite unconsciously. Where does your family invest and are you getting the return that you hope for? The Family ROI Experience is designed to be fun and rewarding, enabling you to achieve an amazing return on your investment of time, energy, and love in your family.

> "Don't say you don't have enough time. You have exactly the same number of hours per day that were given to Helen Keller, Pasteur, Michelangelo, Mother Teresa, Leonardo da Vinci, Thomas Jefferson, and Albert Einstein."
>
> —*Life's Little Instruction Book,*
> compiled by H. Jackson Brown, Jr.

A foreign concept

This can sound like a foreign concept. It's easy to think of family life in the same way that you think about the weather— unconsciously behaving as if your home life is guided by fate or other distant forces, but not by your own intentions—or lack of them. Most people would laugh at the idea of a business plan for your family.

Yet most of us wouldn't dream of being so passive in other areas of our lives. For example, think about your last vacation. How much time did you spend researching the right destination, including where you stayed and the activities you enjoyed? Or when it was time to buy a new television? Strange as it may seem, many probably spend more time comparison shopping for a new computer or video camera than they will ever spend consciously designing their family lives.

Successful organizations ensure their success—so can families

Successful organizations leave nothing to chance. Their success doesn't just happen. Instead, they plan for it. They set long-term goals. They are thoughtful and deliberate. It is often said that those who fail to plan, essentially plan to fail. Knowing this risk, the best organizations use simple but powerful tools to help their teams get along well, thrive, and achieve their goals.

In our careers as communication and change management professionals, we have helped dozens of the largest global organizations design and execute tools and strategies to achieve their goals. Our work focuses closely on helping leaders articulate the company vision and direction, build strategic plans, improve communications, shape corporate culture, and streamline processes.

> "Other things may change us, but we start and end with the family."
> —Anthony Brandt

Along the way, we've discovered that many of these strategies can apply just as successfully to family life. As mothers and wives, we use them in our own homes. We've taught other families to do the same and seen them bring their dreams to fruition—not just leave them as fantasies that never materialize. In addition to the bigger goals, these strategies also help families improve the flow of their daily lives, increasing order, efficiency, and peace.

Our purpose at Family ROI

All families have their own dreams, whether it involves world travel, making it to college, or just spending more weekends together. Family ROI is devoted to helping all families discover their own power to realize these dreams, whatever they may be. We do this by applying proven business principles to revitalize, focus, and strengthen families.

By completing the Family ROI Experience together, you and your family will:

- Spend time together

- Celebrate the uniqueness of your family

- Create a shared vision of your life

- Make exciting plans for the future

- Discover ways to improve your day-to-day lives

- Have fun!

History and evolution of the Family ROI Experience

Although the initial concept for Family ROI was hatched in 1996, the current program was refined by our extended development team in 2004. A year later, we began conducting the first Family ROI Experience workshops in California. In 2006, the head of the New Zealand Families Commission witnessed the Family ROI program in action and invited us to New Zealand to demonstrate the program. By 2007, the government of New Zealand had adopted the program, and today it is being taught to families there across the country. Over the course of our experiences in both California and New Zealand, we have learned that the Family ROI Experience is applicable and effective for families from all socioeconomic and cultural backgrounds around the world.

The principles are universal

Family ROI is based on universal principles and effective practices. Numerous studies have proven conclusively that families who work to improve their communication, engage in regular family activities, and practice family-building skills reap measurable results.

Especially during a child's adolescence, research shows that healthy, open communication with parents, in addition to close relationships and confidence in parental support, is critical. These studies reveal that teens who have positive relationships with their parents are less likely to smoke, drink, or fight with others. They are also less likely to report symptoms of depression and more likely to report a sense of well-being.[3]

Just like organizations, families are not born with perfect communication capabilities from day one. They can be learned, however. A U.S. Department of Justice study found that families who participated in a program designed to improve these skills showed marked benefits five years later, including reduced drug use and delinquency among the children.[4]

Other findings point to the important role that simple family rituals play in building a strong and cohesive family. One study initially published in 1987 discovered that alcoholism is less likely to be passed along to the next generation when families have a tradition of eating dinner together.[5] A Syracuse University study published in the *Journal of Marriage and the Family* found that family rituals play a protective function for the family. Families with preschoolers who reported more meaningful family rituals also reported more marital satisfaction.[6] Greater family cohesion and satisfaction not only feel better for everyone, but they can also translate to less distress, deviance, and heavy drinking shown by adolescents.[7]

These findings are all the more important given that a broad study by the National Adolescent Health Information Center in the United States showed that many teens say they find it difficult to talk with their parents about things that really bother them. Getting along in a family can be challenging, given the unique perspectives, personalities, and needs of each family member. When children are involved, things can get exponentially more challenging. In fact, a study published in the *Journal of Health and Social Behavior* found that U.S. parents, from those with young children to empty nesters, reported being more miserable than non-parents.[8] Why? Parenting is a tough job.

By putting Family ROI practices into use, many families have dramatically improved their communication and connection with their children and partners, improving their relationships, behavior, and commitment, as well as their own personal satisfaction with their lives.

> "Your family and your love must be cultivated like a garden. Time, effort, and imagination must be summoned constantly to keep any relationship flourishing and growing."
>
> —Jim Rohn,
> inspirational speaker

Family ROI is unique

Family ROI differs from other programs in two ways. First, it draws its tools and strategies from the most effective businesses and organizations in the world, simplifies them, and makes them fun and accessible to families.

Second, unlike some family retreats where parents and kids are separated, Family ROI offers a single program that brings together all members of a family. There are no age or height requirements here—we recognize that everyone, even the smallest child, is an important part of the family, so the Family ROI experience offers a fun approach for everyone to participate together.

> "Call it a clan, call it a network, call it a tribe, call it a family. Whatever you call it, whoever you are, you need one."
>
> —Jane Howard

The Family ROI Experience

Successful organizations know the secret power that lies in knowing who you are, defining where you're headed, and running smooth day-to-day operations. We believe all families can achieve their dreams by following a similar journey. This approach is represented by the Family ROI Tree on the next page.

During the Family ROI Experience, your family will explore four areas together:

- Communication
- **Culture**
- Mission
- **Practices**

Communication forms the roots of the Family ROI Experience. In this section, you'll learn strategies *to communicate clearly and compassionately with one another*. You'll also agree on regular family meetings and other forms of communication to stay connected. Once a family has these foundational tools, it can then successfully move on to other steps in the journey.

The first branch of the tree is **Culture**, which represents *who you are as a family*. In this section, you'll define your core values as a family and create agreements to guide your day-to-day interactions. You'll also choose meaningful traditions and create a shared identity to further strengthen your family bonds.

The second branch of the tree is Mission, which represents *where your family is headed*. In this section, you'll explore your purpose as a family and develop a shared vision, along with concrete steps for making that vision a reality.

The third branch is **Practices**, which represents *how your family lives day to day*. In this section, you'll assess and strengthen your daily operations and ensure all family members have a chance to contribute to the running of the family. You will also learn ways to express appreciation for one another.

How to use this book to strengthen your family

First, as a family, make the decision to invest some time in building and strengthening your family. Commit to doing this as a gift for your family.

Next, mark it on your calendar as sacred and nonnegotiable time. We typically offer the Family ROI Experience as a weekend retreat, where families have two intensive, uninterrupted days to focus on one another. We understand that this isn't practical for some families, given many commitments and obligations. Instead, we find that a simple four-week plan works for many. If that is the case for your family, then this book is for you. Even if you have attended or will attend a Family ROI Experience workshop, this book can be a useful reference both before and after your workshop.

Pick a block of two to three hours—perhaps Friday or Saturday evening—that works for every family member and mark that time as your sacred Family ROI time every week for a month. This modest investment will reap amazing results for your family by the end of the four weeks.

Honor this as a very special time for the family. Eliminate distractions by turning off phones, video games, computers, and the TV.

Then begin. During each week, read one section of the book aloud and complete the activities at the end of each section together.

Week 1	Communication	2 hours
Week 2	Culture	2 hours
Week 3	Mission	2 hours
Week 4	Practices	2 hours

You can also complete this book with other families, as we do at the Family ROI Experience. You can gather with friends or as part of a community. This group structure can provide motivation to complete the program, as well as ongoing support.

Family ROI is for the young and old alike

We firmly believe that designing your family's communication tools, culture, mission, and practices is best done when all family members—young and old—are involved in the process together. That's why the Family ROI Experience is specifically designed to be inclusive and fun for the whole family. Families with children should have no hesitation in involving their kids—we make it easy for children to be a part of the entire experience.

Children who are **nine years and older** will find it fun and engaging to participate with their family throughout all four sections. We include experiential activities and simple discussions that will captivate a child's attention.

Children who are **three through eight years old** will find special Family ROI Kids' Camp activities just for them. (Look for the "Just for Kids" symbol throughout the book.) These include educational craft and play activities that tie into the very same topics that the family is discussing—communication, culture, mission and practices—but translated into language a child can understand.

How we define family

Before we begin, we'd like to share our definition of family. We believe a family is two or more people who are committed to sharing their lives together.

Our approach is apolitical and non-denominational. As such, the Family ROI Experience is not affiliated with any religious or political organizations or agendas. We welcome families of different generations, sizes, sexual orientations, religious or cultural backgrounds, and socioeconomic status. The Family ROI Experience has been proven to fit families of all dimensions. Instead of being one-size-fits-all, this experience is yours to customize. It helps you build the family you aspire to create, whatever that might look like.

Get ready to think differently

While the overall Family ROI Experience is designed to be fun and interactive, it may not always be easy. The different exercises will challenge each and every family member. You are likely to have new insights into yourself and your family members and why you behave as you do. You will be challenged to think—and do things—differently.

If serious challenges exist...

We realize that some families are facing serious problems, from substance abuse to infidelity to illness. These challenges may require help from counselors, doctors, and other experts. In many cases, Family ROI may be able to provide valuable insights during a time of crisis. But if your family is facing serious challenges, we urge you to get the professional help you need in conjunction with, or before beginning, the Family ROI Experience.

Suggested agreements

So that you have the best experience, we suggest that you and your family members pause together for a moment and discuss these suggested agreements:

AGREEMENTS

- **Listen to each other**
- **Keep an open mind**
- **Ensure everyone has a chance to give input**
- **Be patient, loving and compassionate (with yourself and others)**
- **Share contributions and tasks**
- **Have fun!**

The journey begins

We invite you to think of your Family ROI experience as a journey. On pages 4 and 5, you'll find the Family ROI Journey Map that your family can use as you move through each step of the experience. Just as you would use a game board, your family can follow the path and stop at each road sign to complete the corresponding activity in the book. Some families find it fun to use a small game piece to mark their movement on the map.

At the end of each activity, you'll be asked to capture your family's discussion or agreements on the journey map in the designated space. Feel free to write

directly on the map included in the book. Alternatively, you can order a large nylon version of the map at www.familyroi.org.

Regardless of the format you choose, make the map unique to your own family. Write your family name in the airplane banner at the top and attach a family photo in the upper left-hand corner.

At the end of the Family ROI Experience, you will have a completed map that will serve as a visual reminder of your unique journey as a family. Many of our Family ROI alumni hang their journey maps in a prominent spot in their home, to remind them of the family's dreams and steps to get there. In fact, as your family grows and evolves, we recommend reviewing your Family ROI Journey Map regularly and updating it annually. Some choose to make this a special, yearly commitment that family members look forward to.

> "The Journey Map is great because it's actually doing something, not just talking things through."
>
> — Julian Lewis,
> Family ROI attendee when he was 14 years old

Before getting started, gather the following materials:

- A photo of your family to attach to the Family ROI Journey Map
- A small game piece to mark your movement on the Family ROI Journey Map
- Pens
- Paper
- Colored markers
- Music and snacks to ensure everyone is comfortable and relaxed

> "We keep the Journey Map up in the hallway. It reminds us who we are and where we're going."
>
> —Angie Lackey,
> mother of four

If you have children ages three to eight, you will also find the following materials useful:

- Three-ring binder, blank scrapbook, or notebook for each child
- Giraffe and Jackal puppets (These can be homemade or purchased)[9]
- Large paper plates
- Old magazines or clip art
- Construction paper
- Scissors

- Glue
- Stickers
- Wooden dowel or a sturdy stick (check for loose pieces that could cause splinters)
- Miscellaneous craft supplies such as feathers, ribbons, fabric, and other embellishments
- Index cards

You are about to begin a magical journey as a family. Congratulations on making this priceless investment in your family. Let's get started.

Just for Kids: My Family ROI Scrapbook

Help each child start his or her own personal Family ROI scrapbook, which can be used to capture the child's artwork and creations throughout the entire Family ROI Experience.

- Give each child a three-ring binder, unlined notebook, or blank scrapbook
- Find or take the child's picture and place it on front of the scrapbook
- Children can decorate their scrapbook cover with crayons, markers, or stickers

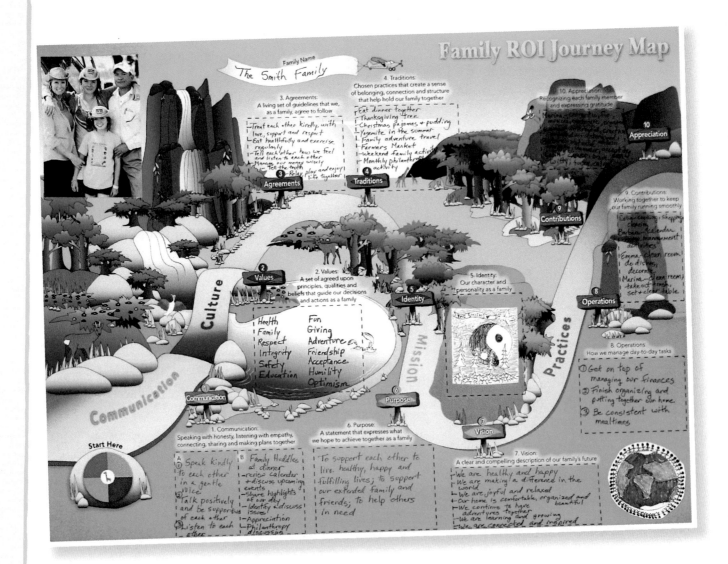

SAMPLE FAMILY ROI JOURNEY MAP

COMMUNICATION

How We Stay Connected

OBJECTIVES

This week, you and your family will:

- Be introduced to a communication process that inspires compassion, connection, and mutual respect
- Practice making observations instead of judgments when you speak
- Understand the importance of identifying everyone's needs—including your own—when communicating
- Learn how to make requests rather than demands
- Agree on communication tools and practices within your family

Communication is core to the success of any organization. Companies invest a lot of time and resources improving how they communicate with customers and employees. They know that without clear, efficient, and effective communication, their business will not run well.

This same principle applies to families. Communication is truly the foundation of every family. We recently heard a story that illustrates this point: A man was walking down the street when he noticed another man struggling with a large washing machine in the doorway of a house. The first man offered to help, and the homeowner was very grateful. For the next six or seven minutes, they struggled mightily with the appliance, grunting and sweating in their efforts. Finally, they were so exhausted they had to stop. When he finally caught his breath, the first man said, "I don't think we'll ever get this

See It in Action

In learning new ways to communicate through Family ROI, the McCarthy family of Rolleston, New Zealand, found the experience has transformed the way they speak to one another, even two years after participating in a Family ROI weekend. "We make sure we take more time to stop and actually listen to what's being said," explained Jacqueline McCarthy, the mother of the family. "Especially with children, it's often not what's being said, it's what's behind the words."

See It in Action

Julian Lewis, from Saratoga, California, completed Family ROI with his family when he was 14. Even though the Lewis family has always been very open with each other, through Family ROI, their habits changed, Julian said. "Instead of getting angry with each other, one of the things we learned was how to really deal with each other in positive, yet still constructive, ways. It's not about telling someone they are wrong, it's, 'How can we do something better?'"

washing machine in the house." And the homeowner replied, "*In* the house? I was trying to move it *out!*"

Compassionate Communication

At Family ROI, we use a communication approach called Compassionate Communication that families find simple yet powerful. Compassionate Communication is a process that strengthens our ability to inspire compassion from others and to respond compassionately to others and ourselves.

It all begins with becoming mindful about how we communicate. Fundamentally, this means becoming aware moment to moment of whether you are:

▶ **Choosing to talk,** *or*
▶ **Choosing to listen**

The most effective communication calls for a balanced flow between talking and listening, between speaking honestly and listening with empathy. This results in shared power, connections, and mutual understanding.

speak with honesty   listen with empathy

The Center for Nonviolent Communication

The Center for Nonviolent Communication (www.cnvc.org) was founded by a man who grew up in a violent inner-city neighborhood in Detroit. That experience inspired him to study peace. Since Marshall B. Rosenberg, PhD, created Nonviolent Communication (NVC), also known as Compassionate Communication, it has been used to quell conflict between warring tribes and within war-torn countries, in schools, homes, prisons, businesses, nonprofit organizations, and government institutions. It's been a catalyst for social change and for the transformation of intimate personal relationships. Today, more than two hundred certified trainers globally teach NVC in their communities.

Jean Morrison (www.communicateforlife.com), a certified NVC trainer based in Santa Cruz, California, helped us adapt NVC specifically for use by families. She is one of the many collaborators who helped build Family ROI.

NVC, or Compassionate Communication, is a reliable language for being heard, for listening to others, for clearly and confidently expressing our needs and dreams, and for working smoothly through conflict. It is sometimes described as "the language of life."

week 1

Try to ask yourself the following questions before any conversation:

- Is it my intention to connect and understand?

or

- Is it my intention to criticize, judge, punish, blame, make wrong, accuse, or interrogate?

In Compassionate Communication, we use two animals to represent these two different approaches to communication.

- We use a giraffe to represent those times when we are seeking to connect and understand.

- We use a jackal to represent those times when we are criticizing, judging, punishing, blaming, making wrong, accusing, or interrogating.

Jackal

- We use the jackal as the symbol for criticizing and creating separation because jackals are known for their skill at attacking. This is why we often call aggressive people jackals.

- The jackal symbolizes that part of ourselves that attacks, runs away, or freezes in panic.

- The jackal uses language such as "You never...", "You should...", "Why do you always...", "Why don't you ever...", "Why can't you...", or "I need you to be..."

Giraffe

- We use the giraffe as a symbol of understanding and connection because it has one of the largest hearts of all land mammals (an average giraffe heart weights 26 pounds).

- The giraffe's height also symbolizes the broad perspective it has.

- A giraffe is tall enough to see everyone's point of view. It takes into account everyone's needs.

- A giraffe is fine-tuned for listening, represented by its big ears and little horns.

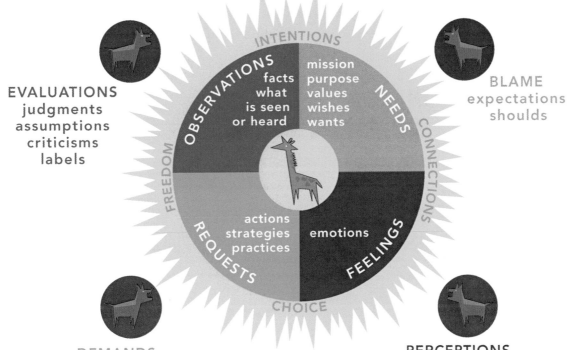

EVALUATIONS
judgments
assumptions
criticisms
labels

BLAME
expectations
shoulds

DEMANDS
no choice
my way
implied or real threat
negative consequence

PERCEPTIONS
thoughts
what I think others
are doing to me
victim language

This illustration summarizes the Compassionate Communication approach. Looking at the inside of the Compassionate Communication circle, you will see that a giraffe communicates by:

- observing
- expressing feelings
- expressing needs
- making requests

Looking at the outside of the Compassionate Communication circle, you will see that a jackal communicates by:

- evaluating
- labeling with perceptions
- blaming
- making demands

week

1

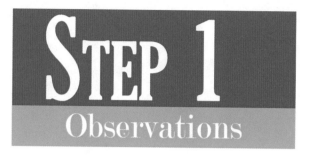

STEP 1
Observations

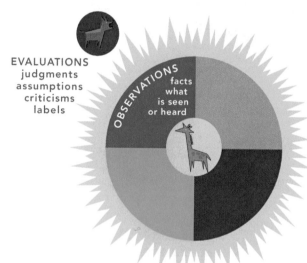

EVALUATIONS
judgments
assumptions
criticisms
labels

OBSERVATIONS facts what is seen or heard

The first step in Compassionate Communication is to observe without evaluating. Pure observation requires us to focus on the facts—what is seen or heard. Most of us don't know how to do this because we haven't been taught how. But it's a surprisingly easy tool to master. Once you develop this skill, it can instantly change the way you communicate and the way your words affect others.

When we use a jackal communication style, we use judgments, criticisms or labels to describe others. To shift into a giraffe communication style, we can make clear, neutral observations about what you see happening. Start by simply naming what you see or hear. Don't evaluate it. Below are a few examples of how to turn a judgment into an observation.

Making observations is the first step towards stronger communications since no person

Judgments (Jackal)	Observations (Giraffe)
Ron is messy, lazy, and disorganized.	Ron's clothes are on the floor.
Rosa is inconsiderate and disrespectful.	Rosa returned the car with the gas gauge on empty.
Rajeen is accomplished and dedicated.	Rajeen completes projects.
Bill is self-centered and always late.	Bill arrives at 9:30 A.M. for 8 A.M. meetings.
Jane is uncreative and boring.	Jane is serving us the same dinner that she served last night.
Jose is stubborn and uncooperative.	Jose stomps his feet and says, "No!"

is judging or being judged. Here are some guidelines to *observing* like a giraffe:

- Report only what a video camera can record, objectively, without interpretation.

- When you speak, be thoughtful and do not rapidly react to what other people say or do. Keep your energy calm, centered, and self-aware.

- Begin with the awareness that both people who are talking are equal players.

Making evaluations can lead to disputes because it involves one person sitting in judgment of another. Here are some clues that reveal you are *evaluating* like a jackal:

- Put a biased lens over the video camera as it records what happens.

- Begin a conversation with the assumption that you are right.

- Sound righteous, viewing the other person not as an equal, but as wrong or less-than.

- Elevate the other person and put yourself down.

- Trigger power struggles and spark arguments.

- Cause distress, antagonism, suspicion, and shame.

Exercise

Take turns having family members read each of the following jackal statements and translate them into giraffe statements instead.

Sample translation:

Jackal: You kids are such slobs!

Giraffe translation: Your clothes and toys are scattered all over the floor.

• • • • • • • • • • • • • • • • • • •

Jackal: Jose is so selfish because he took the last piece of cake.

Giraffe translation: _____

_____

Jackal: Lon works too much.

Giraffe translation: _____

_____

Jackal: You're so irresponsible—you always wait until the last minute to do your homework.

Giraffe translation: _____

_____

Jackal: Jill is negative during meetings.

Giraffe translation: _____

_____

week

1

STEP 2

Feelings

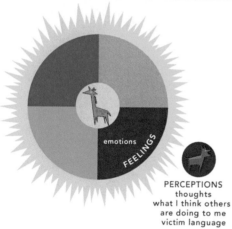

emotions

FEELINGS

PERCEPTIONS
thoughts
what I think others
are doing to me
victim language

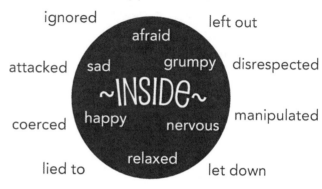

~OUTSIDE~

unappreciated

ignored   left out

afraid

attacked   sad   grumpy   disrespected

~INSIDE~

coerced   happy   nervous   manipulated

lied to   relaxed   let down

made wrong

Once we make an observation about a situation, the second step of Compassionate Communication is to identify and express how we feel about it. Here, we make an important distinction between *feelings* that are just about ourselves and *perceptions* where we blame others for being the cause of our feelings.

> "Two monologues do not make a dialogue."
>
> —Jeff Daly, actor and writer

Inside the purple circle, you'll see examples of feelings: I *feel* sad, scared, happy, grumpy, nervous, relaxed. When we express feelings such as these, we're using a giraffe communication style.

Yet outside the circle, you'll see examples of perceptions of what I *think* you are doing to me: I *think* you're ignoring me, I *think* you're trapping me, I *think* you're tricking me, I *think* you're leaving me out. When we express perceptions such as these, we're using a jackal communication style. These jackal-type phrases put us in a victim role by blaming others as the cause of our feelings.

Giraffe words to describe feelings

Comfortable	Happy	Friendly	Trusting	Interested
rested	glad	warm	open	involved
content	joyful	appreciative	confident	eager
satisfied	cheerful	affectionate	secure	excited
relaxed	delighted	tender	hopeful	curious
refreshed	optimistic	loving	grateful	alert
nourished	proud	compassionate	thankful	inspired
peaceful	ecstatic	sensitive	encouraged	fascinated
relieved	goofy	playful	adventurous	enthusiastic
calm	amused	open	empowered	engaged
tranquil	pleased	sympathetic	centered	stimulated
fulfilled	energetic	touched	safe	intrigued

Discomfort	Sad	Mad	Scared	Confused
uneasy	unhappy	irritable	afraid	indifferent
embarrassed	depressed	frustrated	fearful	troubled
bored	lonely	grumpy	worried	torn
distressed	miserable	irritated	anxious	perplexed
impatient	melancholy	angry	insecure	suspicious
hurt	blue	bitter	helpless	hesitant
restless	gloomy	furious	nervous	puzzled
jealous	sorrowful	resentful	horrified	skeptical
exasperation	regretful	hostile	terrified	shocked
self-conscious	hopeless	enraged	apprehensive	rattled

Jackal words to describe perceptions

attacked	unheard	taken advantage of	taken for granted
ignored	distrusted	bullied	abused
insulted	used	cheated	betrayed
intimidated	violated	coerced	diminished
invalidated	dumped on	misunderstood	interrupted
left-out	disrespected	neglected	misled
let down	put upon	put down	provoked
manipulated	abandoned	unseen	unappreciated
overpowered	blamed	unwanted	unsupported
patronized	harassed	overworked	unimportant
pressured	accused	cornered	invisible
threatened	ripped off	hassled	smothered
trapped	rejected	tricked	deceived

At first glance, you may think the jackal words describe feelings, but, actually, they are perceptions. Jackal words arise from our thoughts or perceptions (our subjective evaluations) of the event or circumstance—they do not represent fact. They describe what we think other people are doing to us. These words are part of a whole body of victim language that implies that another person has power over us.

Have one person in the family read the following statements one at a time. As a family, decide if the statement represents giraffe or jackal language. If it's a jackal statement, all family members can give feedback by howling loudly like a jackal!

		Giraffe Language? ☑	Jackal Language? ☑
1	I feel happy.	☐	☐
2	I feel sad.	☐	☐
3	Are you feeling grumpy?	☐	☐
4	I think you're mean.	☐	☐
5	I feel you're being mean.	☐	☐
6	I feel angry.	☐	☐
7	You make me angry.	☐	☐
8	I feel lonely.	☐	☐
9	I think you're ignoring me.	☐	☐
10	Are you feeling disappointed?	☐	☐
11	Are you feeling confused?	☐	☐
12	I feel satisfied.	☐	☐

Answers   The jackal statements are #4, 5, 7, and 9

STEP 3
Needs

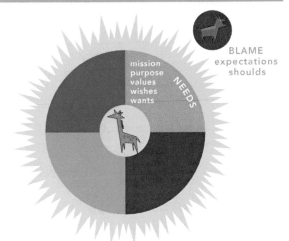

mission
purpose
values
wishes
wants

NEEDS

BLAME
expectations
shoulds

Once we make an observation about a situation and express our feelings, the third step of Compassionate Communication is to express what we need: what we value and what is important to us. Consider the following premise:

> **Anything and everything anyone does is to meet needs.**

Needs are at the root of all of our actions and feelings. If we remember this as we interact with others, this knowledge can help us understand them, no matter what the situation is and no matter who the person may be.

If someone says, "You never understand me," they are really telling us that they have a need for understanding. Their need to be understood is not being fulfilled. If a wife tells her husband, "You're always working—you love work more than you love me," she may really be saying that she has a need for intimacy and would like more closeness and connection.

NVC founder Dr. Marshall Rosenberg believes that "unfortunately, most of us have never been taught to think in terms of needs. We are accustomed to thinking about what's wrong with other people when our needs aren't being fulfilled….If we want coats to be hung up in the closet, we may characterize our children as lazy for leaving them on the couch. Or we may interpret our co-workers as being irresponsible when they don't go about their tasks as we would prefer them to."[10]

Whenever Dr. Rosenberg mediates between two parties having a conflict, he starts by asking two questions:

week

1

- What is it that you each need?
- What would you like to request of the other in relation to these needs?

Once family members can start talking about *what they need* rather than *what's wrong with one another*, the possibility of finding ways to meet everybody's needs is greatly increased.

Think of something you did this morning: fed the cat, vacuumed the carpet, went to the gym, bought a gift for your sister, or screamed when you slammed your thumb in the car door. Now look at the list of basic needs and see if you can discover the needs that were underlying your actions.

Here are some basic, universal human needs that we all share:

Universal human needs

Survival
Air • Food • Water• Shelter • Touch • Sleep

Safety
Security • Protection • Order • Structure • Consistency • Stability

Contribution to Life
Goals • Hope • Purpose • Meaning • Dreams

Belonging
Love • Comfort • Affection • Connection • Appreciation • Acceptance • Companionship • Attention • Sharing • Cooperation • Nature

Trust
Honesty • Reassurance • Support • Integrity

Harmony
Peace • Spiritual Communion • Order

Understanding
Meaning • Exploration • Learning • Experience • Clarity

Consideration
Empathy • Compassion • Acknowledgment • Respect • Warmth

Pleasure
Celebration • Play • Movement • Beauty • Sensuality • Sexuality • Community • Closeness • Intimacy

Health
Exercise • Nutrition • Rest • Space • Time • Movement

Autonomy
Independence • Creativity • Dignity • Freedom to Choose • Confidence • Competence • Ability • Self-expression • Authenticity

Basic needs that children share

Physical Nurturance

Air • Exercise • Food • Protection • Rest • Shelter • Touch • Water

Fun

Play

Learning

Relationship with Our Self

Achievement • Acknowledgment • Being Real • Challenges • Self-worth • Clarity • Competence • Creativity • Integrity • Knowing Our Talents and Gifts • Meaning • Purpose • Privacy • Self-development • Self-expression

Relationship with Others

Appreciation • Belonging • Sharing Life's Joys and Sorrows • Closeness • Community • Consideration • Predictability • Empathy • Emotional Safety • Honesty • Understanding • Interdependence • Kindness • Love • Equal Power • Reassurance • Respect • To Matter to Someone • Trust • Warmth • Friendship

Choices

Relationship with the World

Beauty • Contact with Nature • Harmony • Inspiration • Order • Peace

"Settle one difficulty and you keep a hundred others away."

—Confucius, Chinese philosopher

week

1

See It in Action

Learning how to understand the needs of their children made a huge difference for Barbara and Colin. Their youngest daughter Marina was so full of energy all the time, and they found themselves constantly saying, "Marina, sit down. Marina, be quiet." It was exhausting and frustrating for them—and for Marina.

Once Barbara and Colin began to learn about communicating with compassion, they understood that everything we do is to fill some need we have. In Marina's case, at her young age, she had a tremendous need to move. Her young body needed a lot of activity.

"Instead, we were always trying to get her to conform to our needs for peace, calm, and quiet," Barbara recalled. "It was a very one-sided proposition, which wasn't working!"

So, instead of continuing to try to force Marina to settle down, Barbara and Colin began to honor and support their daughter's need to be active, and so they hung a climbing rope with knots in it from a beam on their living room ceiling. When everyone was together talking or reading, Marina could expend some of her prodigious reserves of energy by climbing up and down the rope.

Once Barbara and Colin made this discovery about their daughter, they no longer thought that she was just trying to be difficult. They could turn their energy to helping meet Marina's need—and they could stop nagging!

"When you become clear about your needs, everything is easier," Barbara said. "This is about making life easier for everyone. It's not about giving away your rights. It's about accepting what is. You can try to control and manipulate, but it will backfire on you."

STEP 4
Requests

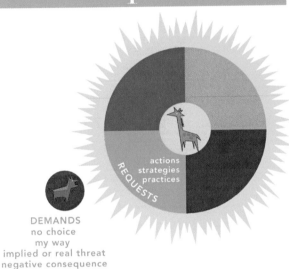

DEMANDS
no choice
my way
implied or real threat
negative consequence

The first three steps of Compassionate Communication involve making observations, expressing feelings, and articulating needs in a way that is not criticizing, analyzing, or blaming. The fourth step entails making requests of others (or ourselves!) for actions that would fulfill our needs or represent our values. The key is to express our requests in a way that others are more willing to respond to our needs.

When we use a jackal communication style, we make demands, which can often invoke fear, rebellion, or submission. In contrast, to shift into a giraffe communication style, we can make requests, which can often inspire respect and cooperation.

Before we make a request, we need to ask ourselves:

- What do I want the person to do?

- What do I want their reasons to be for doing it?

Here are a few examples of giraffe needs and requests:

- I could use some help getting ready for our guests who arrive tonight; would you please sweep the stairs this afternoon?

- For my peace of mind, would you be home by 9 P.M., or call to let me know where you are?

- I need to complete the project. Could you get the report to me by Friday?

- I want to show respect to the performers. Would you please sit quietly beside me?

- Would you tell me how you feel about this situation?

week

1

Giraffe Requests	Jackal Demands

- Specific and concrete, not general and vague
    - They identify something specific the other person could do or say (e.g., "Would you be willing to talk after lunch?," or "Would you help me with my homework this afternoon?").
- Positive language
    - We express the actions that we are requesting, not what we are not requesting.
- Present tense
    - They pertain to the current moment to foster connection and understanding.
- Open to a no
    - A true request implies that we are OK if the person says no, understanding that the other person's needs may be in conflict with it.
- Invitations
    - They invite the other person to honestly share his or her response to the request.
- Based on the premise that the other person's needs are as important as my needs
- Limited
    - Once the request is made, the speaker turns the dialogue over to the other person, in order to listen to and receive what that person is saying.
	- Get others to say yes to what we want
	- Not open to a no ("What I want!")
	- Framed to deny choice to the other person ("Because I said so!")
	- Imply punishment or negative consequence ("Or else!")
	- Fail to take the other person's needs into consideration
	- Try to control the outcome
	- Inflexible and stuck on one strategy
	- Belligerent

Have one person in the family read the following statements one at a time. As a family, decide if the statement represents a giraffe request or a jackal demand. If it's a jackal statement, all family members can give feedback by howling loudly like a jackal!

		Giraffe Language? ☑	Jackal Language? ☑
1	Stop fooling around!	☐	☐
2	I want you to stop drinking.	☐	☐
3	Could you please turn the TV volume down a bit?	☐	☐
4	Why can't you be more helpful?	☐	☐
5	Would you be willing to make dinner for the family tonight?	☐	☐
6	You should put your plate in the dishwasher when you're finished eating.	☐	☐
7	Don't hit your brother.	☐	☐
8	Would you like to do your math homework or practice your piano first?	☐	☐
9	Don't be so selfish.	☐	☐
10	Would you please stop making so much noise?	☐	☐

week 1

Making Requests of Children

Here's a question we hear often: As parents, is everything supposed to be a request when we want our kids to do something? What do we do when something is not open for negotiation?

We have a need to ensure our children are safe. There are going to be situations where we really can't take no for an answer. For example, we wouldn't ask a child, "Would you be willing to wear your seatbelt?," "Are you OK with putting on a helmet before you ride your bike?," or "Would you be willing to not touch that hot stove?" Since we're not open to a no answer, these are not true requests. And that's OK—it's our job as parents to keep our kids safe and healthy. We just need to understand the distinction.

This doesn't mean that it's OK to use a demanding voice when discussing these non-negotiables. In fact, we will be heard more effectively if we practice Compassionate Communication regardless of the topic—whether a request or not. Acknowledging both our needs and our child's needs when talking about topics such as these will go a long way. Instead of "Would you be willing to wear your seatbelt?," we can say respectfully, "Please buckle your seatbelt. I want you to be safe while we're driving."

"A torn jacket is soon mended, but hard words bruise the heart of a child."

—Henry Wadsworth Longfellow, poet

Compassionate Communication overview

Here is a summary of the four steps that your family can follow to ensure you're communicating with compassion:

Step 1 - Observations

Practice making observations; these are neutral statements about what you see or hear without the filters of your own conclusions, opinions, judgments, evaluations, or labels.

Step 2 – Feelings

Share your feelings (emotions) about the situation and listen to the other person's feelings. Be sure you are sharing real feelings rather than thoughts or perceptions.

Step 3 – Needs

Share your needs and listen to the other person's needs. These are not situational needs but basic human needs such as belonging, appreciation, and love.

Step 4 – Requests

Make clear and specific requests, rather than demands, to meet your needs. Requests acknowledge that the other person's needs are as important as yours. Requests are do-able, specific, not attached to an outcome, and open to a no answer.

Resource: Nonviolent Communication (www.cnvc.org)

week

1

See It in Action

Shelley and Abe Smith report that their relationship was borderline dire before participating in a Family ROI weekend in 2006.

Shortly afterwards, Abe told us, "I married Shelley six years ago and we'd been together for more than ten years overall. We got married because we loved each other, but right before we did the Family ROI program, we were not happy at all. Our communication was strained and I didn't care about what was going on with us personally."

Shelley agreed. "Abe and I were losing ourselves and each other. There was no 'us' anymore and there was no 'me' time either. While we are usually both really good communicators, there were lots of 'shoulds' and 'nevers' when we talked to each other. At one point, our son said, 'Mom, Dad, no fighting.' And he's two and a half."

"By practicing Compassionate Communication, our communication at home has been much better. The Family ROI program taught us to define the needs of our family members and how to discuss it," Shelley told us. "We are both better about communicating."

Four years later, we caught up with Abe and Shelley again, to see if some of these changes had stuck. They had. Not long ago, Abe surprised Shelley with a surprise trip to Napa Valley to celebrate their tenth wedding anniversary.

Shelley said, "Abe and I both want to be with each other. There is nothing more important. Family ROI gave us the tools and outlet to deal with our problems."

⏱ 10 Minutes — Activity 1a Communication

1. Move your game piece to #1 *Communication* on the Family ROI Journey Map.

2. Discuss and identify three ways your family can communicate more compassionately.

1 _____
_____
_____

2 _____
_____
_____

3 _____
_____
_____

3. Write them on your Family ROI Journey Map in section #1a marked *Communication*.

Just for Kids: Communication Skits

Review the basics of Compassionate Communication, including the concepts of the giraffe and the jackal. Have your child(ren) practice telling the difference between giraffe and jackal communication.

- Explain the concept of the giraffe and jackal.

- Act out different scenarios or skits. Have the kids identify each scenario as a giraffe and jackal by making the jackal sound when appropriate.

- Ask what they observed. Ask what they think each person in the skit wanted and needed.

- Ask what each person in the skit was probably feeling.

- Ask the kids what request each person in the skit could have made to make things better next time.

Communication Tools and Practices

Now that you've learned a bit more about communicating with compassion, it's time to get down to the day-to-day tactics—making it as easy as possible for busy family members to communicate on a regular basis and stay connected.

Make communication a priority

One of the first steps to ensuring strong communication in your family is to make it a priority. The most successful organizations do not leave communication to chance but put in place tools and practices to ensure it happens effectively. These companies invest in practices such as regular meetings, one-on-ones, and virtual communication tools to ensure people are collaborating effectively to run the business.

Similarly, one of the best practices for families to ensure strong communication is to set up regular methods and times to communicate, such as:

- **Family huddles:** Hold weekly meetings to get together to communicate.

- **Dinnertime conversation:** One family we know had gotten in the habit of watching TV during dinner. At a Family ROI weekend, they realized that their communications with each other had been seriously diminished by this practice because they would become engrossed in the TV and pay little attention to each other. They went back to having dinner at the dining room table and immediately noticed a marked improvement in their communications.

- **Driving time:** Time in the family car, such as when an adult is taking a child to school or after-school activities, can be a good time to talk.

- **One-on-one time between family members:** Most kids appreciate the undivided attention of an adult during special one-on-one opportunities. We know one family who established a simple father-daughter tradition of sharing a Pop-Tart together on Saturday afternoons. It has become their special time to be with one another.

Communication doesn't have to be serious. In fact, some of the best communication happens when families are simply having fun. And having more time for fun as a family is one of the things that Family ROI is ultimately all about.

> "What we speak becomes the house we live in."
>
> —Hafiz, poet

Family huddles

Family meetings or family huddles are a great way to establish an ongoing, positive family connection. Many families use a regular huddle to make decisions, solve problems, or just share the latest news. The key is to have everyone play a part and contribute something.

Family huddles can be planned for the same time each week (e.g., Sunday after dinner).

In addition, any family member can call for a special huddle whenever they feel the need.

The Book of New Family Traditions is a useful resource for how to hold a family huddle. Here are some of author Meg Cox's recommendations for making your huddles great.

Suggestions for Great Family Huddles[11]

1. Everyone gets a say.

2. Start with each person sharing the best thing that happened to him or her that day or week.

3. Go over the upcoming week's events with the family calendar on the table.

4. Take turns leading.

5. State problems without blaming, then brainstorm together.

6. Take five minutes to discuss big-picture questions, such as "Where should we go for summer vacation?," or "Is it time to get a dog?"

7. End with a fun activity or dessert treat.

8. Keep next week's agenda on the refrigerator so anyone can add to it.

9. Use questions that encourage discussion: "Why do you think it is important to…", "How do you feel when…", etc.

10. Think about key issues you want to discuss beforehand. Do research on topics such as drugs or sexuality, if necessary. Be prepared with written notes to make sure certain issues are covered and to keep the talk on track.

11. Use resource materials. Find a video, book, or article that can be used during the huddle to facilitate the discussion and educate everyone.

12. Remind everyone of the family agreements, such as speaking respectfully, not interrupting others, and not making fun of others' ideas.

week

1

Initially, Jacqueline McCarthy of Rolleston, New Zealand, wasn't too excited at the idea of a family meeting. "My first impression was, 'What? A family meeting? We are the parents. We make the decisions.' I was thinking, 'Why do the kids need to have a say?' But, then we realized it wasn't about having power at all. We are still the parents, and we make the decisions. But family meeting are about everyone having their say and feeling listened to."

In Danville, California, Lesli, her husband Stan and their three children find that bedtime is the best time for their family to huddle every night. "There is something about a darkened room and the calm of the evening to get kids to open up," Lesli said. "This is when we hear the most from everyone and when everyone is most receptive to listening." Before saying good-night, each family member shares three good things about the day. It's a way for the family to end the day together on a high note and to remember that something good happens every single day.

Talking stick

Many families, especially those with children, enjoy incorporating a talking stick into their family huddles. Taking turns, whoever is holding the stick has the opportunity to speak. Contrary to its name, a talking stick is also equally about listening. The stick signals when the time has come for other family members to be silent and listen. Try using a talking stick at the beginning of your family huddle to ensure everyone has a chance to share their ideas and feelings.

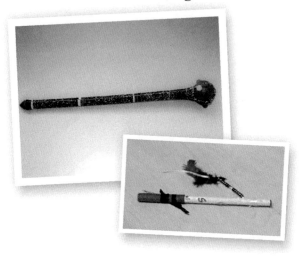

When Native Americans use a talking stick, they sit in a circle. By doing this, no one person is at the head of the table. Instead, everyone is seen as valuable to the conversation. After the first person speaks, he or she can pass the stick. Everyone should have a chance to speak, but at the same time, no one should be forced to share.

The Maori of New Zealand believe a talking stick is charged with the energy of everyone who has ever touched it. The members of the *hui* (gathering) tune into the energy of the others in the group. By doing so, they know instinctively who to pass the talking stick to next. As the speaker receives the talking stick, everyone in the group focuses their energy on the speaker to give him or her clarity of thought and confidence to share an important message.

After attending a Family ROI weekend, the Glover family of San Francisco started to use a talking stick when they held their short daily meetings. Michelle, Jason, and eight-year old Corbin each get to have a say. "We start with the high of the day and the challenges of the day," Michelle said. "You are actually able to listen and learn. I

think it breeds joint respect and provides an opportunity for dialogue with your child."

**Just for Kids:
Communication Skits**

Children can create a talking stick for their family to use during family meetings.

- Siblings can work together to make one stick for the family.

- Find a wooden dowel or a sturdy stick.

- Have the children decorate it as they wish, with simple stickers, ribbons, feathers, or other embellishments that you can find at a local craft store.[12]

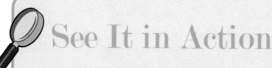

See It in Action

Although they aren't Maori, the McCarthys of New Zealand have found the talking stick to be a powerful tool in their home. They used it after Jacqueline and Frank McCarthy noticed that something was amiss when their 13-year-old son Scott came home from school. "How was your day?" they would ask him. "Fine, fine," he would respond.

But they sensed something was wrong. In fact, for quite some time, another boy had been behaving in a way towards Scott that the school regarded as bullying. Scott didn't want to tell his parents. One day, Jacqueline and Frank had an idea: They handed Scott the talking stick. At first, Scott talked on and on about unrelated things. His parents listened. Feeling more comfortable, he talked some more. They continued to listen. Eventually, in the middle of another story, he said, almost as an aside: "I ran away from a boy at school." Then he tried to change the subject. Eventually, the whole story came out.

Once they knew what was wrong, the McCarthys could help their son—and they did. Today, the McCarthys say Scott talks much more openly with them. He knows they really want to hear what he has to say. "We learned from Family ROI that we needed to stop and listen to each other," Jacqueline said.

Tools to stay connected

Families can also stay connected by using some of the following tools:

- A bulletin board in the house
- E-mail
- Texting and instant messaging
- A family Facebook account
- Shared Excel spreadsheets
- Calendars either generated and maintained on a computer, online, and/or on paper and displayed at home
- Document and calendar sharing applications

Sheryl and Eric Lewis and their two sons use a classic business tool to stay in touch with each other: an Outlook calendar to plot the week. Each family member has his or her own color to indicate scheduling commitments every week. Sheryl sends the calendar via e-mail to her husband and two sons every week so that each family member can see what the others are doing. Grandpa, who lives nearby and helps pick up the boys from school, also receives the calendar with his own responsibilities highlighted in a different color. This weekly e-mail has become a unifying point for the family. All of the family's activities, from the individual to the shared, are laid out on the calendar. Want to know if Dad will be home on Wednesday night? Want to know when Daniel has his Model United Nations competition? Check the schedule. Sheryl also designed an Excel spreadsheet that she uses every week to manage one of the family tasks they struggle to master: meal planning and preparation.

> "Love does not consist in gazing at each other but in looking outward together in the same direction."
>
> —Antoine de Saint-Exupéry,
> French pilot, poet, and author

The Lewis' calendar and spreadsheet for meals make life simpler for everybody in their family. But this may not work as well for your family. Instead, some Family ROI alumni create a family Facebook account where everyone can check in, organize schedules, keep up an online stream-of-conscious dialogue, and share photos. Others use Twitter as a way to stay in touch. And some families prefer more low-tech tools, such as bulletin boards and Post-it notes on the refrigerator. Find a system that works best for you.

Who needs to know?

We've found that the most successful families commit to sharing important information with each other and consciously ask who needs to know what information.

One Family ROI alumnus told us about a weekly carpool schedule that she created, so she and her husband would be in sync about who was responsible for picking up the kids from school each day. She and her husband were pleased that their system to stay in touch was working well. However, during a Family ROI discussion, her 12-year-old son asked, "How come I don't get a copy of the schedule every week, too?" The mom had never considered giving a copy to the son, but in hindsight, he too definitely needed to know the daily schedule! ∎

Activity 1b
Communication

1. Decide when you will hold regular family huddles.

   _____

   _____

2. Review the family huddle guidelines on page 51 and create your own.

   _____

   _____

   _____

   _____

   _____

3. Agree on some basic family huddle agenda topics.

   _____

   _____

   _____

   _____

   _____

   _____

4. Consider using a talking stick as part of your family huddle.

5. Write all of the above on your Family ROI Journey Map in section #1b marked *Communication*.

CULTURE

Who We Are

week 2

OBJECTIVES

This week, you and your family will:

- Define your shared values as a family

- Agree on the behaviors most needed for creating your best family

- Identify your family's most treasured traditions and establish new ones

- Create a symbol to represent the unique identity of your family

What comes to mind when you hear the word culture? Most people tend to think about the different cultures of the world, the unique customs, the clothing, and the food of particular ethnic or national groups. Just as societies have distinct cultures, so do organizations—an invisible quality, style, and a way of doing things. Sometimes people are referring to culture when they talk about an organization's soul.

Boiled down to its bare essentials, culture can be defined as the beliefs and expectations shared by members of a group. Culture may include:

- Philosophy
- Values
- Behaviors
- Language
- Organizational structure

- Agreements for getting along

- How decisions are made

- The feeling or climate conveyed by the way members interact with each other and with outsiders

Research has shown that there is a correlation between strong, well-developed organizational cultures and high financial performance.[13] The most successful organizations know that culture is a powerful factor affecting long-term success, so steps are taken to actively shape it.

Yet most organizations fail to keep a close eye on the company's culture. In fact, approximately 70 percent of large company mergers fail to meet expectations.[14] Most experts agree this occurs because the companies involved do not effectively acknowledge or address the culture issues.[15]

Just like organizations, all families have distinct and powerful cultures, too. Your family has a unique soul—your own way of doing things, your special style, and an invisible quality that may be difficult even for you to put into words. Just as organizations actively shape their cultures, families can, too. Thoughtfully and deliberately shaping your family's culture can accelerate your ability to achieve your best family.

VALUES

Even if you have never taken the time to identify and articulate them, your family has its own values. Values are an indispensable part of every organization's culture. They are the fundamental beliefs that influence everything we do, from guiding our decisions to determining our actions.

To understand the fundamental role that values play in our lives, consider this: If your house caught on fire, what would you grab first as you made your escape? Here's another question: How would you spend your time if you knew you only had six months left to

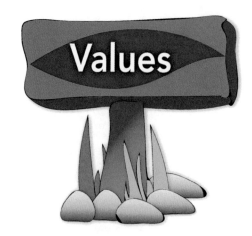

live? Your deeply held values will influence your choices and behavior.

The most successful organizations take the time to identify and articulate their core values. These values then guide their actions and serve as a foundation for their strategies, decisions, and day-to-day actions going forward.

In the same way, families can benefit by openly discussing their values and discerning what is most important to them. Having this clarity and alignment will propel you to build the family you truly desire.

When families are clear about their values and needs and are comfortable with the words used to express them, it is then easier to communicate about situations such as:

- Acknowledging, celebrating, and appreciating when things happen that meet our family's values and needs, or

- Acknowledging, mourning, and making requests for different behavior when things happen that do not meet our family's values and needs.

This orientation towards values and needs is the basis for continued learning and growth by all family members, with understanding and compassion rather than blame and punishment.

It is important to note that there is no one universal set of values. Instead, every family needs to figure out for themselves the values that they believe in. Here are a few examples of values that Family ROI alumni have expressed are important to their families. You will see a more complete list of values in the next activity.

Community	Adventure	Integrity
Stability	Fun	Humor
Generosity	Family	Patience
Conservation	Honesty	Simplicity
Authenticity	Loyalty	Learning
Peace	Respect	Health

Once you've identified your values, the challenge is then to ensure you are living them every day. Families with children know firsthand that kids learn by imitating, especially at a young age. They are adept at seeing the difference between what we do and what we say. If they spot a conflict, they will follow your behavior. As author Robert Fulghum wisely observed, "Don't worry that children never listen to you; worry that they are always watching you."

week

2

20 Minutes

Activity 2
Values

Your first activity for this week focuses on identifying and agreeing on your shared values. This is a time to decide which values are most important to your family.

1. Move your game piece to #2 *Values* on the Family ROI Journey Map.

2. Cut out the values cards on pages 61-76.

3. Together, review the values cards. Use the blank cards if you'd like to add other values. Place the cards into three piles:
   - Most important
   - Important
   - Less important

If anyone in the family feels a value belongs in the *Most Important* category, put it there.

4. Agree on your family's top ten shared values.

   _____

   _____

   _____

   _____

   _____

   _____

   _____

   _____

   _____

   _____

5. Write your family's top ten shared values on your Family ROI Journey Map in section #2 marked *Values*.

6. Assess how your family is currently demonstrating these values.

   a. Give each family member a green and a yellow pen or marker.

   b. Working independently, each person should mark a green dot next to the values that he or she thinks the family is demonstrating well.

   c. Working independently, each person should mark a yellow dot next to the values that he or she thinks the family could improve and demonstrate better.

   d. Once everyone has finished, listen to why each person chose a green or yellow dot. Discuss where the family is most successful and where you could make some changes.

Cut out the following Family ROI values cards.[16]

Acceptance	Accomplishment	**Accountability**
Accuracy	Achievement	Acknowledgment
Adventure	**Affection**	Appreciation
Attention	**Authenticity**	**Balance**
Beauty	Caring	**Celebration**

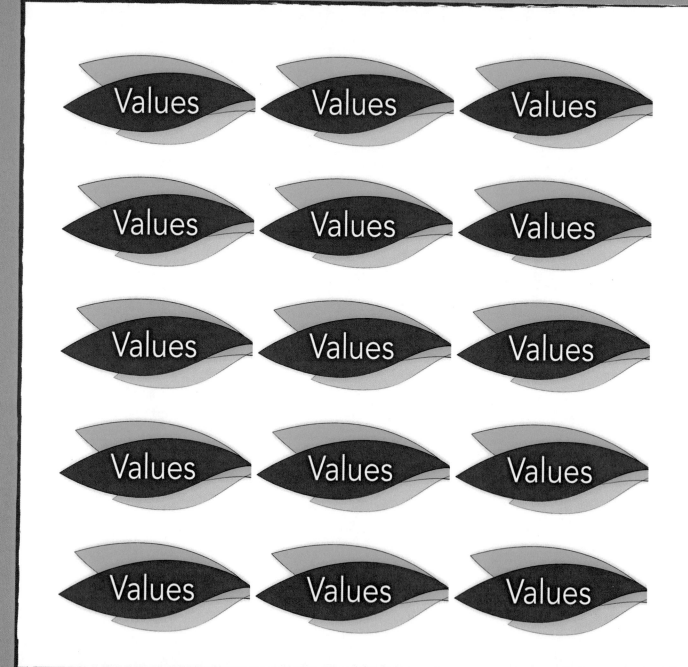

Clarity	Closeness	**Comfort**
Collaboration	Community	Compassion
Competence	**Competitive**	Connection
Conservation	**Consistency**	**Contribution**
Cooperation	Courage	**Creativity**

week 2

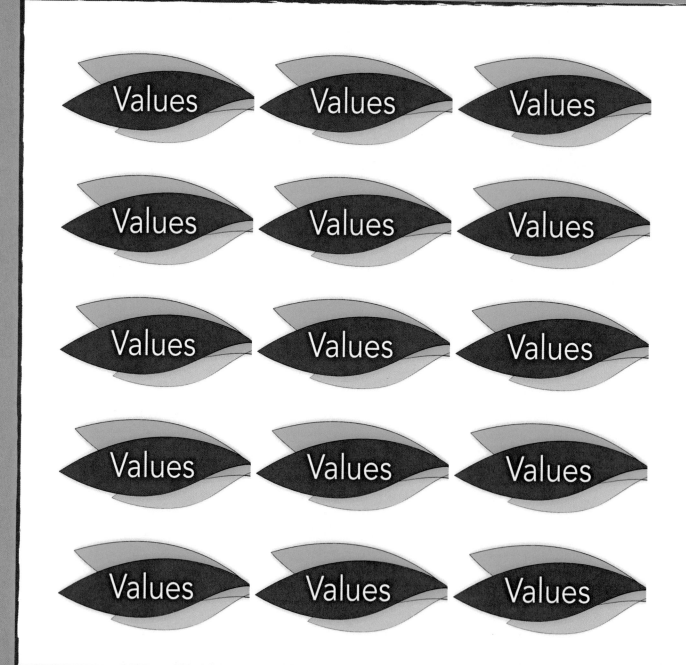

Dignity	Discipline	**Equality**
Empathy	Empowerment	Environment
Excellence	**Excitement**	Exploration
Faith	**Family**	**Flexibility**
Focus	Forgiveness	**Freedom**

week

2

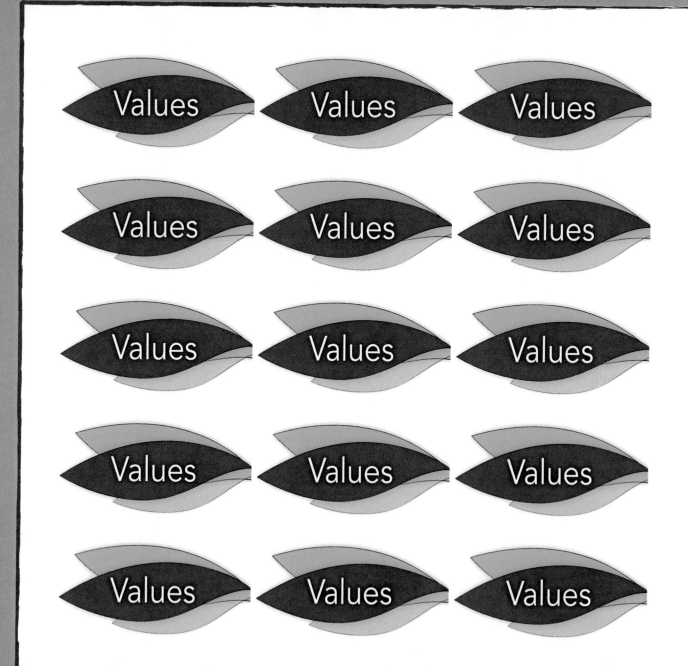

Friendship	Fun	Generosity
Growth	Harmony	Healing
Health	Helpful	Honesty
Honor	Humor	Independence
Innovation	Inspiration	Integrity

week 2

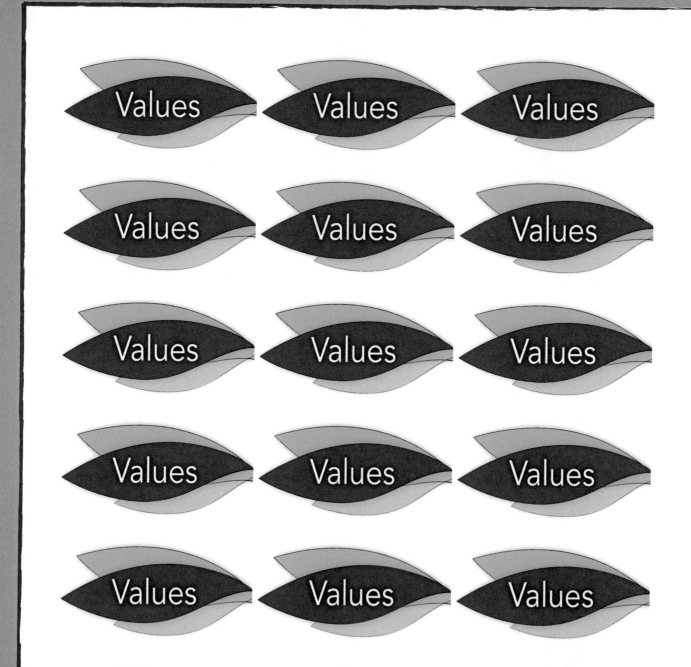

Intimacy	Joy	**Kindness**
Learning	Loyalty	Love
Meaning	**Nature**	Nurturing
Order	**Patience**	**Peace**
Performance	Perseverance	**Play**

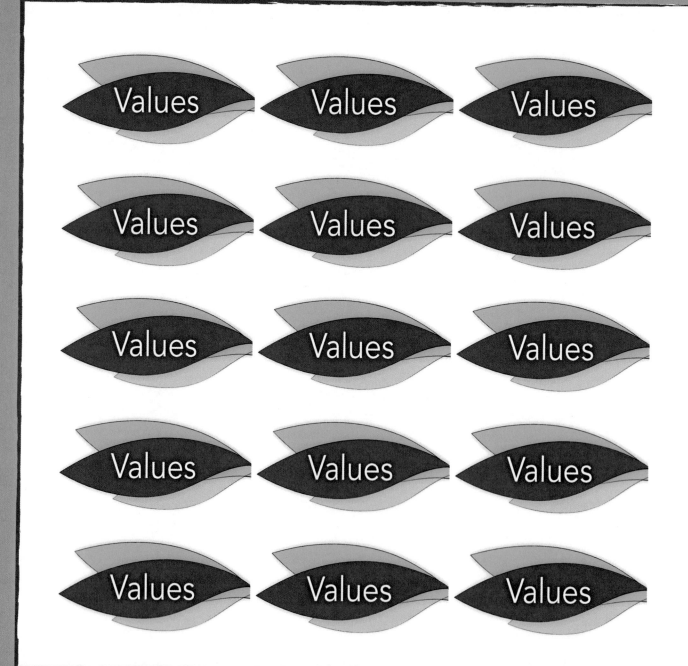

Power	Privacy	**Productivity**
Professionalism	Prosperity	Purpose
Quality	**Recognition**	Recreation
Relationships	**Reliability**	**Respect**
Responsibility	Rest	**Risk-taking**

week

2

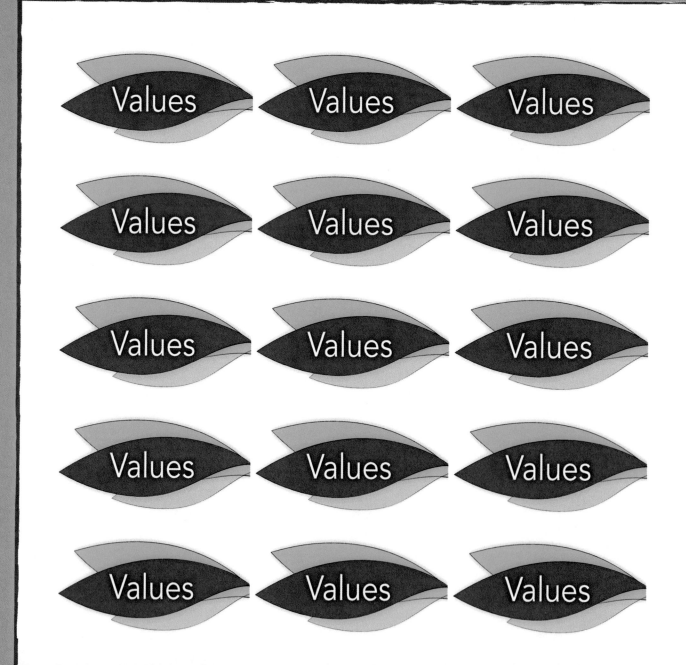

Security	Self-expression	Service
Sharing	Simplicity	Stability
Structure	**Success**	Support
Synergy	**Teamwork**	**Tradition**
Travel	Trustworthiness	**Vitality**

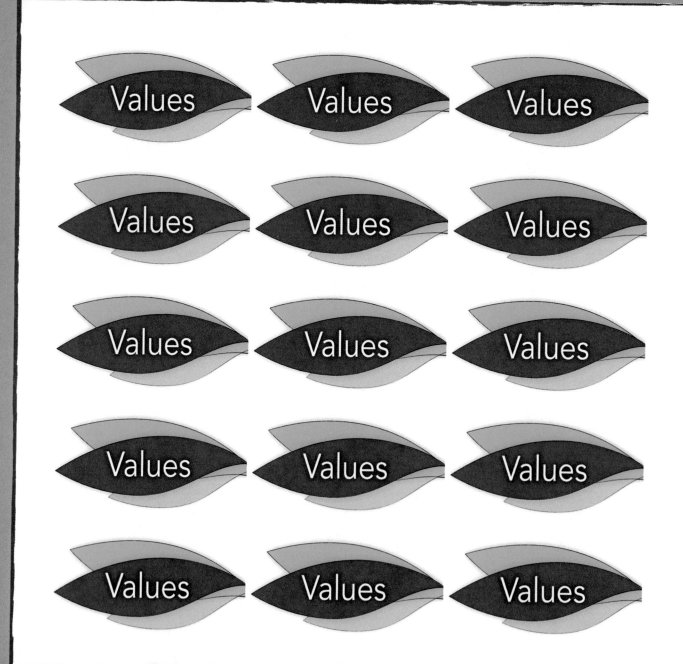

Fill in your own cards if desired.

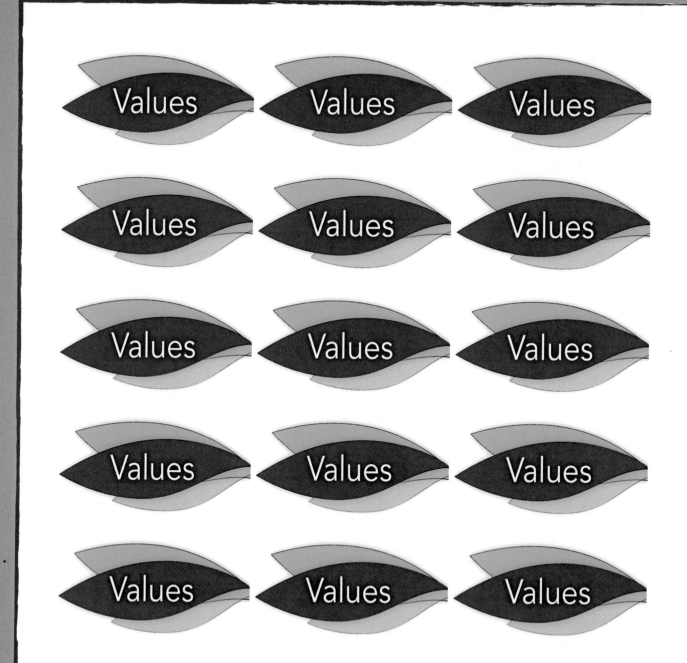

Just for Kids: Values Wheels

Children can think about what is most important and fun to them in their lives.

- Ask each child to think about the most important and fun things or activities in his or her life.

- Help each child to brainstorm a list. The list might include family time, vacations, friends, school, play, fun, rest, food, love, and learning.

- Have each child create a Values Wheel. Write the child's name in the middle of a paper plate and then assign values to what they find most important and create a pie chart on the paper plate.

- Discuss these values briefly with your child or children.

- Insert the plate into their scrapbook when they are finished.

"If you bungle raising your children, I don't think whatever else you do well matters very much."

—Jacqueline Kennedy Onassis,
American First Lady

See It in Action

When the Lackey family of Santa Cruz, California, sat down to look at their values, they ended up spending more time on this discussion than on any other part of the Family ROI program. Each family member felt passionately about which values were and should be most important. One discussion centered on the difference between the words honesty and integrity. After much back and forth, they decided integrity always included honesty. "It took us a long while to get down to those nuggets," said Angie Lackey, the mother of the family. Eventually they settled on: accountability, compassion, faith, forgiveness, integrity, intimacy, love, respect, teamwork, and time with family. They also decided that, as a family, they were doing the best job expressing compassion, faith, and forgiveness.

week 2

See It in Action

The Rivera family finds that when their values are clear and regularly discussed, it's easier to make decisions as a family. "We experience fewer arguments when we're debating what to do, since we have our family's agreed-upon values as our yardstick and objective guidepost," Stan said. When the couple's twin sons were invited to a friend's birthday party, which involved going to see a violent PG 13 movie, they agreed to skip the movie and offered to meet up with their friends afterwards instead.

"It's not hard to make decisions when you know what your values are."

—Roy Disney,
nephew of Walt Disney

AGREEMENTS

At home and at work, what we say never has as much impact as what we do. In fact, a significant part of culture is our behaviors—how we actually do things. While values provide a foundation, they are often too intangible for people to act upon until they also understand the underlying behaviors—what we actually see and hear.

Organizations often set the tone and provide clear clues about how they want employees to behave and perform. Policies and procedures, formal and informal rewards and recognition, and other practices let employees know what behavior is acceptable or not.

In the same way, family members often give one another clues for how they expect each other to behave. Some behaviors are OK in a family and others are not. Imagine how powerful it would be if your family openly discussed and agreed upon which behaviors are helpful—and not helpful—in creating the life you want.

Here are some examples of types of family behaviors:

- How we speak to one another

- How we celebrate successes

- How we spend our money

- How we help one another and others

- How we discuss problems

- How we make decisions

All families have unspoken and spoken agreements for how they want members to behave every day. Sometimes we learn about the unspoken agreements only after we have broken them. Some families explicitly talk about their agreements. Here are examples of agreements that Family ROI alumni have established in their families.

IN OUR FAMILY, WE:

- Treat each other kindly, with love and respect

- Eat healthy foods and exercise often

- Speak calmly

- Tell each other how we feel and listen to each other

- Get ready on time

- Spend our money wisely

- Apologize when we make mistakes

- Tell the truth

- Love each other

- Play and enjoy life together

- Love and respect all people as well as other living creatures and plants

Lisa Stambaugh's family of Fremont, California, observes a couple of overarching agreements. The first is: Tell the truth. The second is: There are no taboo subjects. In other words, the kids get to bring up anything they want. If the subject at hand demands some research, the discussion will be held at a later date—but it will take place.

week 2

Activity 3
Agreements

1. Move your game piece to #3 *Agreements* on the Family ROI Journey Map.

2. Discuss the following questions:

   a. What behaviors do we see in our family that we like?

   b. What behaviors are not acceptable?

   c. What behaviors do we want to change?

3. Develop and agree on your family's agreements.

   a. Give everyone a chance to propose an agreement.

   b. Remind everyone to phrase the agreement as a positive statement such as, "We speak to each other calmly and with respect," instead of, "No yelling." This will provide greater clarity and direction.

4. Write your top agreements below.

   _____
   _____
   _____
   _____
   _____

5. Write your family's agreements on your Family ROI Journey Map in section #3 marked *Agreements*.

This unflinching openness has become well-known among the Stambaugh children's friends who love to come over for dinner and talk about things they aren't allowed to discuss in their own homes. "Sometimes," Lisa said, "the answer is, 'I don't know, but I have a friend who does. Do you want me to call them?'" The only taboo subject is vomit, which is not to be discussed at the dinner table. Otherwise, in the Stambaugh household, it's all fair game!

Just for Kids: Agreements

Discuss with your children the need for agreements in families.

- Ask: What are some agreements in our family?

- Why do we need agreements?

- What could happen if we didn't follow the agreements?

TRADITIONS

Family traditions are a wonderful part of family culture. Traditions and rituals are powerful ways to help you build the family that you want. Each time you carry out a tradition, you provide a structure that connects people to each other and prevents them from drifting apart. Traditions help to reinforce a family's identity by establishing how to communicate with each other, how to make decisions and solve problems—as well as how to celebrate holidays, milestones, and other family events.

Traditions don't need to be complex and time-consuming. Even the simplest rituals,

such as the family dinner, can be powerful. In fact, author Morag Fraser writes about the importance of meal times for the development and support of family life. She describes the family table as one of the "ancient as salt" rituals that serves as "the training grounds of a family, a community, and a civilization." In her own family, Fraser describes that "meal tables were the sites for confession, laughter, revelations of catastrophes, for rites of passage and initiation …. It is around the table…that the family skills and family experiences are to be acquired."[17]

> "Children are the living messages we send to a time we will not see."
>
> —John W. Whitehead, author

The Book of New Family Traditions is a great resource for ideas on starting family traditions. We love author Meg Cox's top ten reasons for why traditions and rituals are important.[18]

Traditions and rituals:

1. Impart a sense of identity
2. Provide comfort and security
3. Help us navigate change

week 2

4. Teach values
5. Pass on ethnic or religious heritage
6. Teach practical skills
7. Solve problems
8. Keep alive the memory of our ancestors
9. Help us heal from loss or trauma
10. Generate wonderful memories

You'll now have a chance, as a family, to talk about the traditions you already observe and to shop around for others you may want to start in the future.

> "A house becomes a home through love and respect among its residents, not from a stylish address or a motto on the wall."
>
> —Ralphe Howland, Jr.,
> inspirational speaker

See It in Action

After reflecting together on what traditions they wanted to initiate, the four members of the Alexander-Hodge family of Alameda, California, decided to nominate their own family holiday. They named it Hawashaha, decided to observe it annually the day after Thanksgiving, and celebrated with lots of candles. It became their special day to relax and unwind and just enjoy each others' company after all the preparations and high spirits of the holiday had passed. Naming it and claiming it together became part of the fun!

Activity 4
Traditions

1. Move your game piece to #4 *Traditions* on the Family ROI Journey Map.

2. Conduct a traditions inventory. Identify the rituals, customs, and traditions that you already have as a family. Write each tradition on a separate index card.

3. Get ideas for possible new traditions.

   a. Take a look at the sample traditions listed on pages 84-87.

   b. Using index cards, have each family member write down any traditions that they like, as well as others that may not be on the list. Write each tradition on a separate index card.

4. Sort the tradition cards.

   a. As a family, shuffle all the index cards together—both the cards with traditions that you already do as a family plus the ones with new ideas.

   b. Have each person flip a card over and read it aloud.

   c. Together, decide whether you want to start, stop, or continue this tradition, as applicable.

   d. Put each card into the appropriate pile. Do the same until you have worked your way through the entire deck of cards.

5. Write the traditions you have agreed to continue and start in the lines below and on your Family ROI Journey Map in section #4 marked *Traditions*.

   _____

   _____

   _____

   _____

   _____

   _____

   _____

   _____

week

2

Sample Traditions

Thanksgiving Tablecloth

Using a white tablecloth and fabric markers, have every family member write what they are grateful for directly on the tablecloth. Kids can also sign their names or trace their hands. Use the same tablecloth every year for Thanksgiving dinner.

Pep Talk in Chalk

Get up extra early on the first day of school and write messages to your child on the sidewalks on his or her way to school. Your kids will enjoy walking along reading *Good Luck!* and *Have Fun!* as they head off for their first day.

Make Way for New Toys

Before birthdays, sort through all existing toys (and clothes) to pull out those things that are no longer used. Donate all the old toys and clothing to a local shelter, or save for the next youngest child to wear.

Report Card Dinners

Create a special dinner when report cards arrive. This isn't to reward good grades, but to celebrate the effort that the kids have made throughout the quarter or semester.

START   STOP   CONTINUE

Tradition Card Sort

Feed the Poor

Some families try to work some part of the Thanksgiving weekend in a soup kitchen, but there are other ways to help as well. One is to buy a duplicate feast: If you're having turkey, buy a second bird; if you're making potatoes, buy a second bag. Pack this feast and deliver it to a local homeless shelter or agency that serves the poor. (Make arrangements for delivery before buying the food.)

Front-Step Photo

Take a picture of your child or children dressed up and ready to head out to the first day of school on your front steps each year. Then, over the years, you can collect these photos together to show the change in the family over time.

Back to School

Each year before your children's first day of school, ask them what they want to be when they grow up. Write the answers on apple-shaped cards made from red construction paper. Paste these cards with each child's goals and dreams in a back to school book along with their annual photo. Your children will love looking back at all of the different dreams they had when they were younger.

See It in Action

The three members of the Glover family of San Francisco decided to change the way they celebrate birthdays. After going through the Family ROI Experience, they decided to take a trip to celebrate four-year-old son Corbin's birthdays. When they do throw a party for him, they urge the other kids to bring toys that Corbin and his parents donate to a local charity called The Hamilton Family Center, which gives them to needy children. "It's inspired Corbin to think about charity differently," his mother Michelle Glover said. Another one of the family's traditions is to hold music parties. Corbin plays the violin and many of his friends play different instruments. When they all come over to the Glover household, they come prepared to play.

Week 2

Teacher Reflections

Ask your child's teacher if he or she is willing to write a short letter to your child at the end of the school year, reflecting on the child's talents, accomplishments, and funny occurrences during the past year. Saving all of the letters over the years will provide wonderful memories for your child.

Conversation in a Jar

One way to get the conversation rolling is to keep a jar in the middle of the kitchen table. Fill the jar with a couple dozen strips of colored paper marked with the sort of questions celebrities get asked. At meals, each family member picks one. Some ideas: *The most surprising thing about me is…*; *Three things that make me happy are…*; and *If I had a million dollars, I would….*

Giving-Back Day

Designate one day each month as a community service day in your family. You can fill activity bags with coloring books, crayons, and games, and deliver them to the local children's hospital. For other possibilities, visit a local nursing home and read to elderly residents; bake cookies and deliver them to the local fire or police station; or sign up to help clean a nearby park or hiking trail.

Dates with Dad or Mom

Set aside one night or afternoon a week for a special date with your kids. If possible, make it one-on-one time, perhaps alternating whose turn it is each week. Let the child dictate the activity each week, whether it's playing catch, bowling, or visiting a local hobby store. Even when your work life is busy and insane, this allows you to keep a special time to reconnect with your child each week.

See It in Action

During the holidays, Lesli and Stan Rivera's family started a tradition that they call "Our Advent Books" to help the three children count down the days to Christmas. They individually wrap 25 Christmas-themed books—some old favorites and some brand-new—and number them from 1 to 25. Each day, the family opens up a book to read together in the evening. It also provides a peaceful break every evening during a busy season.

Bedtime Countdown

Keep a checklist of all the pre-bedtime tasks that need to be completed such as brushing teeth or collecting stuffed animals. That way, as the kids are getting ready, you can call out *check* as each item is completed. After the last item, the lights are turned out.

Goodnight Family Tree

Say goodnight to all the people your child loves. The names may change over the years as friends change or with new teachers, but it is a great way to remind children about relatives who they may not see very often. Be sure to include aunts and uncles, cousins, babysitters, and grandparents, too.

Family Game Night

Pick one night a week reserved for family games. Family members take turns picking what game(s) to play and what special foods or drinks to enjoy.

Sample traditions excerpted from *The Book of New Family Traditions* by Meg Cox.

One Tradition that Pays Off: The Family Dinner

Teens who have infrequent family dinners (fewer than three per week) are twice as likely than teens who have frequent family dinners (five or more per week) to use tobacco or marijuana; more than one and a half times likelier to use alcohol; and twice as likely to try drugs in the future, according to a report by The National Center on Addiction and Substance Abuse (CASA) at Columbia University. "The magic of the family dinner comes not from the food on the plate but from who's at the table and what's happening there. The emotional and social benefits that come from family dinners are priceless," said Elizabeth Planet, CASA's vice president and director of special projects.[19]

week

2

IDENTITY

Successful organizations spend a lot of time developing their identities, which represent their brands. Coca-Cola, HP, Microsoft, Rolex, Disney, Nokia, and Google are just a few of the well-known companies appearing on Interbrand's 2009 Best Global Brands List.[20] A unique identity and a great brand are powerful forces that differentiate companies from competitors. They also help to forge an emotional connection with customers and ignite the loyalty and passion of their employees.

A brand identity is carefully crafted to communicate the essence of the product or

organization and symbolize what makes it unique. Specifically, an identity:

- Defines products, services, and organizations in a recognizable way
- Reinforces purpose and values
- Symbolizes uniqueness and often evokes an emotional connection

You can probably think of many companies who have developed instantly recognizable brand identities. How many of these slogans can you identify?

- A diamond is forever
- Just do it
- The pause that refreshes
- The ultimate driving machine
- The world on time

Answers   De Beers, Nike, Coca-Cola, BMW, and FedEx.

Most families don't have logos or slogans, but they used to. In fact, during the Middle Ages, a form of family branding was quite prevalent, as knights used a coat of arms to differentiate themselves from others. In a full coat of armor, each solder looked a lot like the others, so the coat of arms was used to identify a knight in battle—a label that provided instant identification. On a battlefield, knowing the identity of every solider you encountered was a matter of life or death.

Developing a coat of arms or a brand identity for your family is a fun way to create a visual representation of your family and what you are all about. It can also create a stronger sense of connection, belonging, and loyalty.

> "We worry about what a child will become tomorrow, yet we forget that he is someone today."
>
> —Stacia Tauscher,
> author

See It in Action

The four members of Leslye Alexander's family of Alameda, California, wanted to create more balance in their lives. So they chose a yin-yang symbol for their family crest. The Simpson family of Westlake Village, California, chose a compass, which serves to remind them that whatever they do in their lives as individuals or together, they want to remember to put family and religion first. Because they live on a street with the name Rose in it, a picture of a rose sits at the center of the compass. Right now a picture of their crest hangs on their refrigerator. One day, they hope to have their family symbol carved in wood and mounted in the center of their living room on the wall.

week 2

Activity 5
Identity

Now you'll have a chance to create a symbol of your family's identity. Your family may prefer to use a family crest; a modern logo; or even a motto, slogan, or jingle. You can use visual, written, or spoken elements—or a combination of all three.

There are no rules to this—the only criteria is that all family members must play a part in creating the family's brand identity.

1. Move your game piece to #5 *Identity* on the Family ROI Journey Map.

2. Discuss your family's unique identity by answering the following questions:

a. What do we love about our family?

_____

_____

_____

_____

b. How is our family unique?

_____

_____

_____

_____

_____

_____

_____

_____

_____

_____

Activity 5
Identity (continued)

c. What do we want to tell the world about our family?

_____

_____

_____

_____

_____

_____

_____

_____

_____

3. Brainstorm key elements that appeal to you as a family, which could be used for your family brand identity.

  a. Take a look at the sample family logos on pages 92-93 and images on pages 95-96, to get ideas and get your creativity flowing.

  b. Select and cut out any images that especially appeal to family members. Choose a few or as many as you like. You may also want to search on the internet or skim through magazines for graphics that you like.

4. Create your family brand identity.

  a. As a family, agree on how you would like to represent your family's brand identity, either as a family crest, logo, jingle, slogan, motto, or some other visual or literary form.

  b. Draw or write your family brand identity.

5. Write or paste your family brand identity on your Family ROI Journey Map in section #5 marked *Identity*.

Week 2

"Home is where the great are small and
the small are great."

—Author Unknown

"What really binds people together is their culture, the ideas, and the standards they have in common."

—Ruth Benedict,
anthropologist

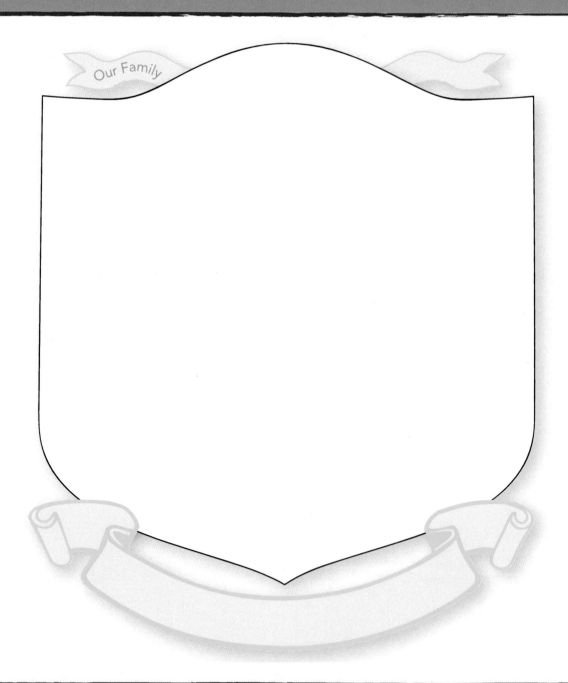

Our Family

week 2

MISSION

Where We're Going

OBJECTIVES

This week, you and your family will:

- Define your purpose and vision as a family
- Develop an action plan to achieve your vision

The most successful organizations in the world know why they exist and what they're all about. They have a clear sense of their mission—understanding where they want to go, how they're going to get there, and what they'll do when they arrive.

In contrast, poorly performing organizations get so caught up in the day-to-day work of running the business that they neglect investing time in planning for the future. Employees are often in reactive mode, spending time fighting immediate crises rather than proactively moving towards carefully chosen goals.

week 3

Families often replicate this same dynamic. Do you get caught up in the pressing needs of each passing day without taking time to identify where you want to end up one year, three years or five years from now? Do you often feel like you're spending so much time and energy just getting through your day that it's impossible to focus on the bigger picture?

In our fast-paced world, many families face these challenges. But without a clear and specific understanding of who you are and where you are going, families risk drifting aimlessly and ending up on a rocky shore, rather than in the port of their choice. As American author and speaker Zig Ziglar aptly commented, "If you aim at nothing, you'll hit it every time."

The good news is that families, like successful organizations, can use simple strategic planning tools to get off the treadmill and create a path toward achieving their most-cherished dreams. A simplified approach to family strategic planning includes:

- Articulating your family's purpose
- Creating a clear vision of your desired future

PURPOSE

A clear and common purpose makes all the difference in an organization. As a result, people become well-aligned and act consistently and decisively.

> "The purpose of life is a life of purpose."
> —Robert Byrne,
> author and billiards champion

Nikos Mourkogiannis, leadership expert and author of *Purpose: The Starting Point of Great Companies*, believes a clear purpose can be used to inspire and lead an organization to greatness. He says, "When a company or foundation is driven by … a shared purpose, … morale will be higher, … quality of innovation will improve, … relationships will be strengthened, and … leaders will be able to point the way forward with genuine conviction."

High-performing organizations know their reason for being. And it's not just about making money. Mourkogiannis explains that "many of the most enduringly successful companies have been driven by something beyond profits, such as discovering new things, helping other people, producing excellence, or becoming the best player in their industry."

For instance, Henry Ford's original ambition was to "democratize the automobile." Sony's founder explicitly said the "joy of technological innovation" was one of the reasons for the company's existence. Nike co-founder Bill Bowerman viewed endless possibilities for human potential in sports when he created a company whose mission is "to bring inspiration and innovation to every athlete in the world."

Just as an organization's purpose statement can harness the energy and talents of its people, a family purpose statement can unify, inspire, and bring out the best in your family. It doesn't need to be poetic or worthy of publication—just a heartfelt description of why the family exists.

> "He is happiest, be he king or peasant, who finds peace in his home."
>
> —Johann Wolfgang von Goethe,
> German dramatist, novelist, poet, and scientist

A family purpose statement can be ambitious or down-to-earth. For instance, the McCarthy family of Rolleston, New Zealand, wanted to focus on the basics when crafting their family's purpose statement. They chose, "To listen to each other, improve our communication, and live in greater harmony together." Similarly, the Lackey family decided on "To be nice, do the right things, and help others when able." Angie Lackey explained, "For us, that was kind of our bottom line."

week

3

sample Family Purpose statements

Here are sample family purpose statements shared by some Family ROI alumni. A purpose statement can be as simple or elaborate as you want.

- To support each other to live healthy, happy, and fulfilling lives; to support our extended family in times of need; to help others in need.
- To be there for one another.
- Create a place of order, truth, love, happiness, and relaxation; to provide opportunities for each person to become responsible, independent, and effectively interdependent in order to achieve worthwhile purposes.
- Our family purpose is to create a nurturing, safe environment that:
    - honors individual differences
    - creates giants out of self and others
    - encourages spiritual, emotional, and physical development
    - role models loving relationships
    - promotes caring, open communication
    - makes a positive, joyful difference in our inner and outer worlds

A good purpose statement expresses what you hope to achieve together. It should be consistent with your family's values and resonate with everyone in the family. Ideally, all family members will say, "Yes, this is what I'd like our family to bring to life at home and within our sphere of influence. This is how I'd like others to know us."

"A palace without affection is a hovel, and the meanest hut with love in it is a palace for the soul."

—Robert G. Ingersoll, poet and political leader

Activity 6
Purpose

1. Move your game piece to #6 *Purpose* on the Family ROI Journey Map.

2. Review your values in Activity #2 since they should serve as a foundation for your purpose statement.

3. Talk with your family members about the following questions:

   a. What is important to us as a family?

   _____

   _____

   _____

   _____

   b. What do we want to achieve as a family?

   _____

   _____

   _____

   _____

   _____

   c. What is our purpose together?

   _____

   _____

   _____

   _____

   _____

4. Given what you have just discussed, decide on and write your family purpose statement below.

   _____

   _____

   _____

   _____

   _____

   _____

   _____

5. On the Family ROI Journey Map, write your purpose statement in Section #6 marked *Purpose*.

week

3

VISION

Taking the time as a family to articulate a vision can be a powerful catalyst for change. Once we know where we are and have a vision of where we want to go, it's easier for us to keep on track as we move forward.

A vision is a clear, concise, and compelling description of what you want things to be like within a certain period of time. It describes what your destination looks and feels like, and provides important context when planning for the future.

The first step in figuring out where you want to go is to understand where you are and what your present situation is. To develop your vision and a plan for reaching it, you'll work together on four steps:

1 Define where you are today and where you want to go

2 Identify how far you are today from your vision

3 Prioritize

4 Create an action plan

During Family ROI Experiences, we've heard families share an amazing diversity of dreams. Some include the following:

- Starting a family
- Traveling to see the world
- Moving to a new area or fixing up your home
- Taking a sabbatical from work
- Being able to work from home
- Spending more quiet days at home

- Learning to fly an airplane
- Going back to school
- Working part-time
- Adopting a baby
- Slowing down
- Volunteering
- Running a marathon or completing a triathlon
- Making a career change
- Learning a new language
- Writing a memoir
- Having a family game night or activity night once a week

The Lackey family of Santa Cruz, California, found themselves discovering a vision that surprised all of them. As a result, they ended up going somewhere called Club Mud—not the fancy resort Club Med, but something else entirely—all because of their vision discussion during a Family ROI weekend.

Angie Lackey, the mother of the family, surprised her husband and children when she told them, "It has always been my dream to work with the poorest of the poor." No one knew she felt that way. Life at home was so busy with four children and her husband Nate's work as a fireman, that Angie figured

week 3

she simply wouldn't get the chance to realize her dream in this lifetime. But once she said it out loud, she and her family began talking about how they might find a way to make her wish come true.

> "One day Alice came to a fork in the road and saw a Cheshire cat in a tree. 'Which road do I take?' she asked. His response was a question: 'Where do you want to go?' 'I don't know,' Alice answered. 'Then,' said the cat, 'it doesn't matter.'"
>
> —Lewis Carroll,
> author of *Alice's Adventures in Wonderland*

A year later, Angie found herself traveling with her two oldest children to Tecate, Mexico, where they spent a week building permanent homes for families so poor that they live in makeshift shelters or out in the open. The experience was so powerful for the Lackey family that the whole family returned to Mexico the next summer through the same program called Club Mud. In a couple of years, Angie and her two oldest children will travel to India where they will be trained in basic dental cleaning and work together at an orphanage, serving the children and the surrounding community.

"I am not an assertive person," Angie said. "So, without Family ROI, this never would have happened because I never would have stepped up and said how important this was for me." But she did. And it turns out that the fulfillment of Angie's vision has had a profound effect not only on the people the Lackeys have helped, but on the Lackeys themselves.

Setting goals together during a Family ROI weekend also had a profound effect on the Alexander-Hodge family from Alameda, California. Griff had inherited a farm from his family in Wales. Periodically, he and his family would go there for vacation. They dreamed of living there one day, but didn't think it could be done, given demands at home. Both Leslye and Griff work as full-time teachers.

But once they realized everyone in the family shared this dream, they made it an explicit goal. Both Leslye and Griff secured six-month sabbaticals from their jobs. They packed up their kids and realized their most far-fetched dream of living in the Welsh countryside for six months. "Just talking about it was very powerful," Leslye said.

Activity 7a
Sharing Dreams

Now it is your turn to reflect on your dreams—both as a family and as individuals.

1. Move your game piece to #7 *Vision* on the Family ROI Journey Map.

2. Have one person read the instructions below aloud, while all other family members close their eyes and listen.

3. Let everyone sit quietly to reflect. Then have each person write down their individual answers to the questions.

4. Once everyone is done writing, share your answers with one another.

Imagine that you are in a place that you love and where you are very comfortable. Imagine yourself there, feeling very relaxed. Now take a few deep breaths and continue to relax and enjoy this beautiful place.

Think about something that you've always dreamed of doing, either on your own or with others.

Imagine that you can do anything you dream of. What would you do?

Another way to think about this is to consider the following: At the end of your life, what will you regret not having done, seen, or achieved? You may find yourself thinking about where you might travel, what career you might choose, what your home life might look like, your hopes for your children, or any other accomplishments.

If you are a child, it might be an activity you'd like to do with your family. Or a dream you have about your future.

Now open your eyes and take a moment to write down some of the ideas that came to mind, then share your dreams with each other.

Notes from sharing:

_____

_____

_____

_____

week

3

See It in Action

Tauha and Gayle Te Kani from Gisborne, New Zealand, developed a vision centered around their life at home. They decided they wanted their home atmosphere to be "lovely and stress-free." They also wanted to spend time every day enriching their relationship by going on walks together, playing music, and just talking with one another.

Earlier, when they were working on the Communication section of the Family ROI Experience, Gayle shared something with Tauha that he didn't know: "You spend so much time watching sports on TV that I feel left out." Tauha was taken by surprise. He didn't know that his favorite hobby was having this effect on his wife. When their five sons were still at home, Tauha loved watching sports with them, as often as he could. But by now, they had all moved out.

"I thought that 'communication' was when we were all sitting in front of the TV together," Tauha confessed. One day, in response to Gayle's concern, Tauha turned off the TV so he could spend more time with his wife. Over time, he started doing so more often. "It didn't happen straight away but now we rarely have the TV on anymore. Gradually we learned how to just sit and talk," Tauha said. Eventually, he even gave up his satellite TV subscription. This choice wouldn't work for all sports fans, but it did for Tauha, who found his choice liberating.

"I don't miss it at all," he said. "My brothers can't believe it because I was a bit of a sports nut." He describes this change as surprisingly life-altering. "Now home is my favorite place. It's my sanctuary. The results of doing this for our relationship are…oh gosh! I should have done it ages ago."

Just for Kids:
Dreams and Wishes

Children can express their wishes or dreams.

- Ask your child to imagine that a genie has magically appeared and offered to grant one wish.

- Invite your child to share one special dream or wish that they have for themselves or their family in the future.

See It in Action

For Greg and Moira Simpson, goal-setting enabled them to achieve their dream of buying a home. About ten years ago, the couple used to spend their weekends paddling outrigger canoes with friends and driving far away to different coastal cities to compete. But after they sat down and looked carefully at their desire to buy a home, they made some changes. They identified a savings rate which would allow them to buy a home in five years' time. Achieving clarity made it easy for them to dramatically cut back on their sport, which was expensive to pursue. They also identified the town about an hour away where they wanted to buy their home. So they both set about finding jobs in the new town so they would be ready when the time came to move. "We had to really cut back on socializing," Moira said. "But we reached our goal and had plenty of money—it was big."

One of their newest goals is to convert their garage into a "man cave" where their son can hang out with friends as he gets older—and give his parents a little more breathing space in their cozy 1,300-square-foot home. They're not sure precisely how they will do but having set and reached many goals together before, they're confident they will.

week 3

35 Minutes

Activity 7b
Envisioning the Future and Assessing the Present

1.   Imagine that it is three years from now and you are very happy with your family life. What does it look like? What dreams and wishes of yours have come true? Write your answers below.

     It is the year_____ (three years from now). Dreams and wishes that have come true:

     _____

     _____

2.   Consider the following 12 aspects of family life from the perspective of each family member.

3.   Discuss your present situation and identify what's working well in addition to problem areas. Write your answers below.

4.   Then imagine it is three years from now and you are very happy with each aspect of your family life. What does it look like? Write your answers below.

1 Physical environment (where you live and spend time—in the office, the family home, the car)

Present_____

_____

Future_____

_____

2 Physical selves (exercise, health)

Present_____

_____

Future_____

_____

Activity 7b (continued)
Envisioning the Future and Assessing the Present

3 Spiritual lives (religious activities, community, meditation)

Present _____

_____

Future _____

_____

4 Relationships (between adults, adult(s) and child(ren), extended family and friends)

Present _____

_____

Future _____

_____

5 Family time (your mornings together, evenings, weekends, vacations)

Present _____

_____

Future _____

_____

6 Daily life (meal preparation, laundry, home care, chores)

Present _____

_____

Future _____

_____

7 Social life (gatherings with friends, parties you throw and attend, events you attend)

Present _____

_____

Future _____

_____

Week 3

Activity 7b (continued)
Envisioning the Future and Assessing the Present

8 Work and school life

Present _____

_____

Future _____

_____

9 Community service (volunteer and charity work)

Present _____

_____

Future _____

_____

10 Personal enrichment (each family member's personal time, including hobbies or after-school activities)

Present _____

_____

Future _____

_____

11 Family finances

Present _____

_____

Future _____

_____

12 Other

Present _____

_____

Future _____

_____

Sample of Activity 7b
Envisioning the Future and Assessing the Present

2 Physical selves (exercise, health)

Present   We try to eat healthy food, but often don't take the time to cook and we don't have a regular exercise routine.

Future   We are eating healthy food, cooking good dinners four times a week, and exercising regularly.

4 Relationships (between adults, adult(s) and child(ren), extended family and friends)

Present   We don't have enough time for each other. We don't go on dates and just relax together.

Future   We go on dates every week and keep weekends open so we have time to just hang out.

6 Daily life (meal preparation, laundry, home care, chores)

Present   Our lives feel chaotic day to day. Our house is often a mess. The laundry isn't done regularly.

Future   Our lives are running smoothly. Mornings are organized. We make a weekly schedule to plan meals.

week 3

Activity 7c
Analyzing the Gap

How far are you today from your vision?

1. Estimate on a scale of 1 to 10 how close you are to realizing your vision in each of the 12 aspects of family life. 1 means your family is very far away from your vision. 10 means your vision is already a reality.

2. Mark your estimate in the circle on the next page. Imagine that the center of the circle represents zero and the outer edge represents 10.

3. Connect the dots and shade in the gap to visually see the difference between where you are and where you want to be.

Note: The main purpose of this activity is to get a general sense of the family's biggest gaps and to become aware of each person's perspective. It is not necessary to reach unanimous agreement on the score for each area. You can compromise. For example, if one person thinks it's a 4 and another thinks it's an 8, call it a 6.

Activity 7c
Analyzing the Gap

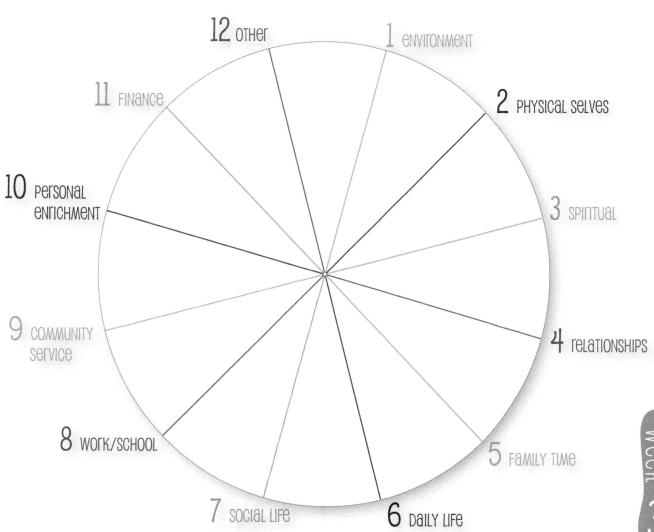

sample of completed chart

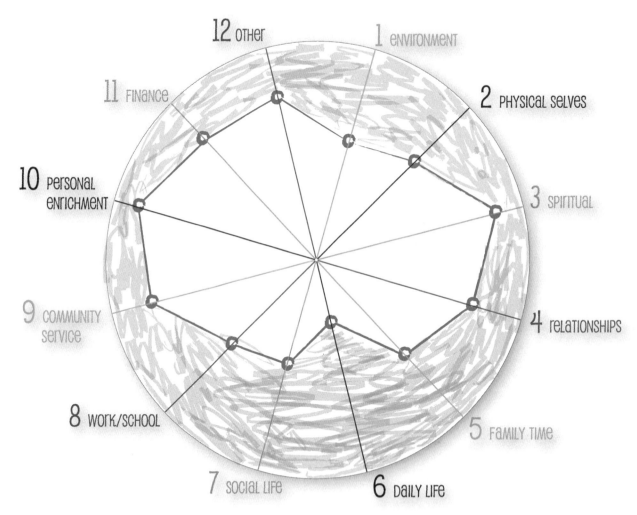

 The blue shaded area represents the gap between where you are today and where you want to be in the future. This chart highlights areas of opportunity where your family can work together to make your vision a reality.

10
Minutes

Activity 7d
Prioritizing Elements of Your Vision

1. Looking at your circle graph, identify the top three areas that need the most attention right now. They may or may not be the ones with the biggest gap.

2. Summarize the key elements of your vision and write it on your Family ROI Journey Map in section #7 marked *Vision*.

1 _____

_____

_____

2 _____

_____

_____

3 _____

_____

_____

_____

_____

_____

_____

_____

_____

_____

_____

_____

_____

_____

week 3

Activity 7e
Action Planning

1. List the actions for each vision area of focus.

2. Identify who will be responsible for each action and when it will be done. Keep things simple and manageable by picking just a few things that have the biggest impact. Consider the following:

   a. What are the steps to move us closer to our vision?

   b. Who will own each step?

   c. When will it be completed?

Sample of Activity 7e
Action Plan

Area of Focus		ACTION	WHO	BY WHEN
1	Physical Selves – exercise regularly	1 Go for a walk after dinner as a family	Family / Mom	Monday–Friday
		2 Repair our bikes	Dad	April 20
		3 Plan fun, active family outing for each weekend	Rotate every week	Every Sunday

An action plan template can be downloaded from www.familyroi.org.

Activity 7e
Action Plan

	ACTION	WHO	BY WHEN
1 Area of Focus	1		
	2		
	3		
2 Area of Focus	1		
	2		
	3		
3 Area of Focus	1		
	2		
	3		

week 3

Activity 7e
Action Plan (continued)

		ACTION	WHO	BY WHEN
4 Area of Focus		1		
		2		
		3		
5 Area of Focus		1		
		2		
		3		
6 Area of Focus		1		
		2		
		3		

See It in Action

When the Rivera family's boys were in kindergarten, Stan and the kids gave Lesli a small photo album for her birthday. Lesli recalls, "When I opened it, I saw that it was empty—there were no photos. However, next to each photo slot, there was a different handwritten caption. Captions such as 'Eating a hot dog in NYC,' 'Seeing a baseball game at Fenway,' 'Climbing the Leaning Tower of Pisa,' 'Learning how to swim,' and 'Going on a cruise with our grandparents.' I was surprised because these were all things that we hadn't ever done!"

The kids explained that Daddy had asked them to talk about all the dreams that they had—both big and small—and then he wrote them down in the album. The plan, they explained, was that the photo album would be filled in together as a family. "It was a reverse photo album where instead of looking back, we were looking ahead. I loved it!" said Lesli.

It was a wonderful gift that the Rivera family has had fun filling ever since. In the last four years, they've eaten lots of hot dogs in New York City, cheered for the Red Sox at Fenway, climbed the Leaning Tower of Pisa, splashed happily in the pool, and cruised with the grandparents!

At an early age, Stan had taught the kids the power of visioning and intention. As the title of one of Lesli's favorite books appropriately promises: *Write It Down, Make It Happen*.

Just for Kids: Journey of Dreams

Children can create pictures of their dreams and wishes for the future.

- Ask each child to think about what he or she wants to be when they get older and some of the things they want to do.
- Help them think about what they would need to be able to realize their dreams. What are some tools they need? What are the skills they need? How can they get them?

- Give each child a piece of paper with a large drawing of an empty suitcase. Provide some old magazines, scissors and glue. Tell them to "pack" for the future, by cutting out pictures or drawing what they need for their journey to do all they want to do with their lives.
- Have them glue or draw pictures inside the suitcase.
- Insert the paper into their scrapbook when they are finished.

week 3

See It in Action

Barbara and Colin Smith were amazed when they first acknowledged and shared their dreams with each other. They couldn't believe that after being married for five years (at the time), there were some very important things they didn't know about each other. Once they did learn each other's dreams, they helped make those dreams a reality. Now thirteen years later, they are still dreaming, sharing, and helping make their dreams and their children's dreams come true. "It doesn't always happen the way we initially imagine it, or in the same time period, but when we share our wishes and put intention behind them, miracles continue to happen," said Barbara.

FAMILY VISION BOARDS

Another fun activity you can do both individually and as a family is to create vision boards. Every December, the Smith family creates vision boards for each family member and then one for the whole family.

Here is a step-by-step approach:

1. Answer this question individually: *Imagine it is the end of the year, and it has been a fantastic year. What has happened?*

2. Write down key words and phrases that capture your thoughts, e.g., straight A's in school, a part in the school play, consistent exercise, travel to South America, etc.

3. Search the internet for images that represent those words.

4. Create a montage of images and words that capture your dream vision for the year (these can be drawn by hand or printed out and put on a poster board, or they can be created electronically).

5. Share your individual vision boards with each other, and go through the exercise together as a family to create a combined vision board.

6. Hang your boards in a prominent spot in your home to remind you of your vision for the year.

Now that your family has voiced your vision for the future and created an action plan to get there, you are well on your way to making it a reality. ■

VISION BOARD

VISION BOARD

PRACTICES

How We Live Day to Day

This week, you and your family will:

- Identify tools to help you manage your family's operational tasks more effectively
- Agree on areas that need improvement and develop an action plan
- Identify how family members can contribute to the day-to-day operations of your family
- Recognize and appreciate each family member's talents

What makes a truly successful organization? Many people think a visionary leader or an amazing product is the key to a successful enterprise. While these are essential, they are insufficient by themselves. Unless an organization pays close attention to its operations—how it actually gets things done day by day—it won't reach its full potential.

In an organization, tasks might include managing employees, building products, controlling the budget, purchasing supplies, and maintaining the building. Devoting attention to all of these activities is important—it is also a lot to balance. Poor execution on operations has led to the downfall of many organizations, including those with great products.

Jim Collins, author and former Stanford professor, emphasizes this point in his book *Good to Great*. In it, he says, "No matter how dramatic the end result, good-to-great transformations never happened in one fell

week 4

swoop. There was not a single defining action, no grand program, no one killer innovation, no solitary lucky break…. Good to great comes about step by step, action by action, decision by decision."

In the same way, running a family successfully is a tremendous job that requires us to pay close attention to day-to-day operations. Many families today complain of a frenetic pace of life, with too much time spent on routine errands and not enough time on the things family members really want to do.

Imagine how families could free up time and energy to pursue their vision if they were able to handle their daily tasks as flawlessly as highly successful organizations do.

The key is to find what works best for you and your own family. There is no one right answer or model.

When one family from California sat down together during a Family ROI weekend to examine their family practices and tasks, they found a stark reality confronting them.

See It in Action

For Greg and Moira Simpson, the process of analyzing their household practices gave them a leg up in an impromptu round of The Newlywed Game that they played with some neighbors. Apparently, the other couples hadn't discussed the division of work in their homes as clearly as Greg and Moira had. When the other couples were asked, separately, how much of the housework their spouse did, their answers conflicted. But Moira and Greg had no such concern. They had discussed the matter thoroughly and constructed their days accordingly long beforehand. So, when Moira was asked how much housework Greg did in their home, she answered truthfully: 100 percent. Separately, Greg came back with the same answer. Moira spends more time with their son and working outdoors in the garden. "We didn't care about making some kind of impression," Moira said. "Everyone thought I would say Greg did 10 percent, but he really does all of it. And we're completely comfortable with that. A lot of people could benefit by going through this process."

There it sat in black and white where they had written it on paper: one person—the mother—was shouldering the lion's share of the duties in the family. No one—not even she—realized this until they examined their daily schedules carefully. Finally, the mother understood why she was having unexplained panic attacks and why she once called the hospital terrified that she was having a heart attack. *I want a new life,* she thought as she reviewed the exhausting details of her daily life. To cool off and absorb the realization, she had to go for a walk alone.

After her husband and their two daughters understood the situation, she got the new life she wanted. All four members of the family began sharing tasks more equitably. Many years later, this same mother wondered if, gone unchecked, the imbalance in the home might have lead to the destruction of her marriage. Not so much because she resented being overworked, but because she now believes, her own acute sense of unhappiness was poisoning the family.

"We felt we had a good life," she said, "and didn't need to do this exercise. We were awestruck by what we got out of it. It makes you look at a part of your life that you put a veneer over." After two years of sharing chores, she now says her family life is much more relaxed and happy today because everyone understands why they need to pitch in. "This process helped me to communicate in a way that was nonthreatening," she added. "It's definitely given me a nice way to say to my family, 'Help.'"

> "You can't do it all yourself. Don't be afraid to rely on others to help you accomplish your goals."
>
> —Oprah Winfrey, television host

week 4

OPERATIONS

Very simply, operations refer to how an organization runs day to day. This can include all the ongoing tasks required to keep the organization running smoothly and accomplishing its goals.

Think for a moment about some of the organizations you interact with. These might include your child's school, the corner drugstore where you pick up your prescriptions, the gym where you work out, or the online retailer where you buy books or download music. Each of these organizations has to manage and coordinate numerous tasks and processes to keep things running smoothly for you. This might include:

- Planning
- Designing products and services
- Providing customer service
- Purchasing materials and supplies
- Maintaining equipment
- Managing employees
- Budgeting and accounting
- Marketing
- Distributing products and services

Thinking about the experiences that you've had with these organizations, which ones have delivered high-quality customer service, excellent products, and/or consistent results every time you've interacted with them? Which organizations have you had a poor experience with? Why? It's very likely that the problems you've experienced can be attributed to poor operations.

A few organizations that are widely known for their superior operations include Amazon, Apple, McDonalds, FedEx, and Ritz Carlton. Each earned their distinctive reputation, whether for efficiency, innovation, consistency, timeliness, or superior customer service, by paying close attention to their daily business operations. It may appear seamless to outsiders, but a lot of time

and attention is devoted to the most basic and foundational practices that keep the organization running like clockwork.

Just as every organization requires excellent operations to survive and succeed, so do families. The tasks that make up the daily life of most families are numerous and can include:

- Cleaning the house
- Cooking and serving meals
- Doing laundry
- Managing the budget
- Paying bills
- Preparing tax returns
- Shopping for food and household supplies
- Planning the family schedule
- Staying in touch with family and friends

 ## See It in Action

By examining their family's daily tasks, the Lewis family of Saratoga, California, felt empowered to make a few needed changes. For a long time, the family members recognized they had a problem with clutter. Sheryl and her husband had even hired a professional organizer to help straighten up the household. The youngest son Daniel hated the clutter ("I lost things all the time"). But Daniel, who was 11 when he attended a Family ROI weekend, wasn't sure what to do about it. After all four family members did some

writing about the clutter while examining their family practices, something shifted. "Before Family ROI, it was this nebulous thing," Daniel recalled. "After Family ROI," he said, "I saw that this was something we could tackle together."

Daniel started looking at the clutter in a different way. Before it seemed like a phenomenon disconnected from him. "Afterwards it was like, this room belongs to everyone and this stuff belongs to everyone," he said. Daniel found himself doing more than he had before to clean the house.

week 4

What Is Mom Worth?

Lest anyone belittle a mom's contributions at home, consider this: The time and talent stay-at-home mothers spend performing the ten most popular tasks of motherhood should command an annual salary of $117,856, according to a recent study by Salary.com. For their part, working mothers should earn $71,860 above their regular salaries for their mom duties, the study also found.

For the past decade, Salary.com has been calculating the estimated market value of a mom's contributions to the family.

To arrive at the 2010 figures, the company surveyed 28,000 moms and quantified the hours they work in more than ten different "jobs" every week. These jobs include laundry machine operator, janitor, van driver, computer operator, housekeeper, day care center teacher, cook, chief executive officer, psychologist, and facilities manager. These responsibilities were then weighted to calculate overall compensation.[21]

At Family ROI, we've discovered that when all members of the family help to shoulder the tasks many mothers perform solo, increased sanity and happiness result, not just for moms, but for everyone else, too.

"Many hands make light work."

—John Heywood, playwright and poet

Many of these tasks are predictable and repetitive—we know how to do them and when they need to happen. They are also essential and necessary. Pretending they are not there will not make them go away. Some are capable of disrupting family life if neglected or done poorly. And all can promise better relationships and free up more quality family time, if done well.

> "Dig a well before you are thirsty."
>
> —Chinese Proverb

In fact, smooth family operations not only make daily life smoother, but they have also been found to result in better health and performance in school. A study published in the *Journal of Family Psychology* found that "in families with predictable routines, children had fewer respiratory illnesses and better overall health, and they performed better in elementary school." The research also found that family rituals have a positive effect on emotional health, with adolescents reporting a stronger sense of self, couples citing happier marriages, and children having greater interaction with their grandparents.[22]

How well does your family run day to day? The next activity can help identify what's working and what's not.

Activity 8
Operations

20 Minutes

1. Move your game piece to #8 *Contributions* on the Journey Map.

2. Review the Operations List on pages 130-131. Add any of your family's key activities that are missing.

3. Have each family member use a colored marker to place a dot next to relevant tasks, according to the following color code:

   a. Green: This activity is running exceptionally well

   b. Yellow: This activity is running well, but could run better

   c. Red: This activity needs to be fixed now.

4. Agree on your family's top three "hot spots"—the most critical tasks with room for improvement. Write them below and in the Family ROI Journey Map section #8 marked *Operations*.

HOTSPOT

1_____

2_____

3_____

WEEK 4

Family & Social Activities

Plan family outings

Plan social events (birthday parties, dinner parties)

Plan vacations

Call relatives and friends

Make gifts/cards

Take pictures

Create photo albums/slide shows

Schedule date nights

Send cards (thank you, birthday, and holidays)

Other

Outdoor Maintenance

Maintain yard (mow lawn, rake leaves, shovel snow)

Maintain garden (pull weeds, plant vegetables)

Maintain major outdoor projects (landscaping, building play structures, putting up fences)

Maintain and repair car(s)

Wash car(s)

Make or coordinate home improvements (carpentry, painting, roofing)

Clean gutters

Other

Shopping and Errands

Buy groceries

Run errands

Buy household supplies

Buy clothing and shoes

Make large purchases (car, TV)

Buy gifts

Take items to dry cleaner

Other

Scheduling

Maintain family calendar/schedule

Coordinate family and work hours

Plan family meetings

Schedule appointments at home (repair services, housecleaners, deliveries) and be available

Schedule classes, workshops, after-school activities

Other

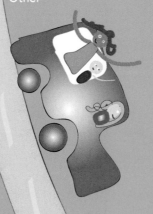

Finances

Plan budget and debt management

Pay bills

Prepare taxes

Manage retirement planning

Manage savings and plan for large purchases (car, education)

Manage insurance, wills, and living trusts

Other

Food Preparation and Cleanup

Plan meals

Make breakfast

Make or pack school lunches

Cook dinner

Wash dishes

Baking, canning or other special food projects

Other

WELLNESS

Schedule doctor, dentist, and other wellness care appointments

Create exercise routine

Lead/organize spiritual practices

Plan stress management activities

Participate in hobbies and personal enrichment

Schedule personal grooming (haircuts)

Other

PET CARE

Feed pet(s)

Play with pet(s) and/or take pet(s) for walk

Take pet(s) to vet

Other

INDOOR MAINTENANCE

Straighten up the house, put things away

Clean the house (dust, vacuum, sweep, clean bathrooms)

Take out garbage

Wash laundry

Prepare for guests

Decorate house (regular ongoing projects)

Decorate for holidays or special occasions

Do small repairs around the house

Manage computers and technology (purchase, maintenance)

Organize and restock emergency kit (fire, earthquake, tornado, hurricane, tsunami)

Manage organizational projects (clean closets, garage)

Plan and practice emergency and safety procedures

Other

CHILD AND ELDER CARE

Feed

Bathe

Transport to doctor, dentist, or orthodontist

Transport to activities

Play and read to/with

Manage morning routine

Manage evening routine

Get up at night

Plan and attend activities

Coordinate, participate in school activities (PTA, sports, coach, club advisor, college visits)

Help with homework

Help learn new skills

Manage behavior and discipline

Other

> "In all things, success depends upon previous preparation, and without such preparation, there is sure to be failure."
>
> —Confucius,
> Chinese philosopher

Tools to help run day-to-day life

Families seeking smoother day-to-day tasks might consider adopting tools commonly used by businesses to run their tasks. Some of these tools include:

- Governance
- Planning
- Budgets
- Processes
- Outside support

Governance (how we manage our operations)

Since every family consists of unique individuals with diverse needs and perspectives, conflict is inevitable in all families. Some structure is needed to help manage the family and ensure shared understanding of how things work. Governance can help to provide an overall framework and processes:

- Agreements and policies
  - How we spend our time
  - How we care for children and elders
  - How we ensure each other's health and safety
  - How we manage spending
- Decision making
  - How decisions are made
  - Who is involved in which decisions
- Roles
  - Who is responsible for doing what

> "It takes as much energy to wish as it does to plan."
>
> —Eleanor Roosevelt,
> American author and First Lady

Planning

Author Lester Robert Bittel once said, "Good planning helps to make elusive dreams come true." Making plans—and following through on them—is critical to making everyday tasks run smoothly, as well as accomplishing long-term family goals. Any project, large or small, can benefit from upfront planning. Creating a simple plan to achieve a goal is the first step to making it a reality.

> "To put the world right in order, we must first put the nation in order; to put the nation in order, we must first put the family in order; to put the family in order, we must first cultivate our personal life; we must first set our hearts right."
>
> —Confucius,
> Chinese philosopher

For kids especially, sitting down to examine the family plans and tasks together can be an eye-opening experience.

Here are some examples of tasks that can benefit from upfront planning:

- Weekly Tasks
    - Meals and shopping
    - Weekend and social events
    - Homework and school projects
    - Exercise regime
    - Taking care of pets
- Monthly and Quarterly Tasks
    - Doctor visits, haircuts, and other self-care appointments
    - Social events
    - After-school and other extra-curricular activities
    - Auto care and service
    - Bill paying and management of household finances
    - Seasonal home care
    - Planting a vegetable garden
- Annual Tasks
    - Sending out holiday cards and letters
    - Preparing tax returns
    - Planning vacations
    - Planning summer activities for children (childcare, swim lessons, camps)
    - Planning birthday celebrations

See It in Action

In New Zealand, Jacqueline McCarthy said that her two children experienced a revelation when their family participated in a Family ROI weekend. Jacqueline recalls, "They realized, 'Oh, we are a part of this family and we need to contribute.'"

Week 4

See It in Action

Julian Lewis was 14 when he participated in a Family ROI weekend with his parents and younger brother Daniel. The Lewis brothers had always performed chores at home, but they hadn't understood precisely why doing them was so important. After Family ROI, Julian said, their attitude "shifted from, 'Do your own chores,' to, 'When you see somebody who needs help—contribute.' It was a realization that more things would be required of my brother and me. It was almost like I didn't realize my potential before. Before, we would do chores separately. I learned that it's so much more fun to do them together. Now, when my mom cooks, I set the table."

Julian also said, "Before Family ROI, I took my parents for granted as the people who cared for me. Afterwards, I started paying much more attention to them as people and as adults. That was really shocking for me."

Budget

Successful organizations use budgets to ensure money is being spent in the best way to keep things moving forward in a sustainable, positive direction. Budgets help organizations know where money is being spent and when certain items cost more or less than originally envisioned.

> "Even the highest tower begins from the ground."
>
> —Chinese Proverb

Similarly, successful families often use budgets for the same reasons: to help keep expenses in line with expectations and to help achieve their financial goals. A budget (also known as a spending plan) is not a financial straitjacket, but rather a tool that lets one spend without worry or guilt.

Creating a budget involves the following steps:

- Analyze the current situation
  - Add assets, debts, income and spending
  - Review attitudes about money

- Identify sources of conflict around finances within the family
- Identify goals
  - College, retirement, vacation home, potential job changes
  - Protection against adversity with six month reserves, insurance policies, etc.
- Develop a plan and stick to it
  - Take action to reach savings, investment, and retirement goals
  - Buy insurance policies
  - Conduct estate planning
  - Institute tax strategies

Processes

Some of the best-run organizations rely heavily on superb process management. Putting rigorous processes in place helps ensure we perform tasks consistently and efficiently, minimizing human error and overlooked details. Most organizational processes are heavily documented and followed carefully. Families can also adopt the spirit of this disciplined approach to process by using informal plans and checklists for some of the family's routine operations. Some family operational tasks that can benefit from a checklist include:

The Top Reason Couples Fight

Consider this: A Relationships Services study entitled "Dealing with Disagreements" found that money is one of the top reasons couples fight, with 41 percent of respondents reporting recurring disagreements about money and financial issues.[23] In addition, a Utah State University study found that couples who reported disagreeing about finances once a week were more than 30 percent more likely to get divorced than couples who reported disagreeing about finances a few times a month.[24] One way to alleviate this conflict is to openly discuss one another's expectations about finances and agree on and follow a budget.

week

4

- Grocery shopping: Make a grocery list before going to the store

- Doing homework: Keep track of homework assignments and projects

- Meal planning: Create a calendar with meals planned for the week or month

- House maintenance: Create a maintenance schedule and list of important contact information for electricians, plumbers, and other professionals

- Weekly plan: Plan the week's activities for the family, including individual and shared activities

- Chore charts: Build a chart that divides chores among all family members

Outside support

With so much to do, and so many demands on our time, it makes sense to consider using outside resources to support our families in achieving our goals. This allows family members to focus on those items that are most important to them. It reduces stress and brings additional expertise to the family when needed. Outside support may require hiring professional experts or creating bartering relationships. It may also mean asking for help from friends and family.

Outside support may come in different categories:

- Daily support
  - Childcare
  - Eldercare
  - Gardening and landscaping
  - Housecleaning
  - Personal training
  - Meal preparation
  - Pool maintenance
- Occasional support
  - Lawyer
  - Accountant
  - Painting and decorating
  - Tutoring
  - Computer expert
  - Financial planner
  - Caterer
- Problem-solving support
  - Family counseling
  - Spiritual or religious advisor
  - Life coach
- Informal advisors
  - Friends
  - Extended family

See It in Action

Daniel Lewis, who was 11 when he first participated in Family ROI, said, "I learned a lot about how my parents run the house. Having a family is a lot more complicated than I thought it would be. Before, I didn't even understand what was going on. I didn't understand what all was involved in running a household. It was right before my eyes, but I wasn't seeing it. Children don't have an opportunity to take part in the family if they don't know what's going on. It's gotta be a team effort. There were huge gaps in my understanding." After Family ROI, everyone had a better understanding of the contributions made by each family member. And they reached some new and creative solutions.

"The one thing that plagued us was meal planning," Sheryl Lewis recalled. "We all highlighted it as a big issue. Each day, we said, 'What shall we eat today?' Then we'd grab frozen food, eat out a lot, and have a headache about it every day."

However, they realized that Daniel had talents that were not being utilized. Sheryl said about Daniel, "He would cook dinner every night if I let him." Today, Daniel cooks often for his family. Some of his specialties include Chinese beef and broccoli, Chinese chicken salad, and an asparagus soup that takes him three hours to prepare.

Sheryl says, "It's great. I love it! Now Daniel likes helping out. [Cooking] is a bond we have."

Before Family ROI, Daniel's responsibilities were to take out the garbage and to set the table. After Family ROI, he said, "I felt like we were doing it all together."

Sharing tasks with family, friends, and neighbors can save everyone time and money. A babysitting circle where two or more families take turns babysitting for the other so the adults can go out together is a great way to save on babysitting costs. Taking turns with neighbors to do gardening or other household chores gets tasks done faster and may even become a fun event. Be creative!

"Live within your harvest."

—Persian Proverb

CONTRIBUTIONS

The most successful organizations are ones that recognize, leverage, and nurture the unique contributions of each individual.

Similarly, a strong family encourages each family member to contribute according to his or her unique capabilities and gifts. Even young children can have, and take great pride in, assigned roles within the family (such as sorting socks or setting the table). Family tasks can be shared among family members in such a way that each person feels as if he or she is making a unique contribution to the success of the family.

"Nothing is particularly hard if you divide it into small jobs."

—Ray Kroc,
founder, McDonald's Corporation

This may include allowing family members to:

- Use their best talents

- Take part in problem solving

- Choose the tasks they most enjoy doing when possible

- Recognize and appreciate work that might otherwise go unacknowledged

- Learn how to take on progressively more responsibility with age

- Learn how to plan for and delegate parts of a complex task

- Celebrate the uniqueness of each person

"Tell me, I'll forget. Show me, I may remember. But involve me and I'll understand."

—Chinese Proverb

Activity 9
Contributions

1. Move your game piece to #9 *Contributions* on the Journey Map.

2. Briefly discuss the following questions and write the answers in the space below:

   a. What are each family member's best talents and skills?

Name of family member	Talents and skills

   b. What unique contributions do we each make to our family operations?

Name of family member	Unique contributions to family operations

   c. How can each of us use our talents and skills to help build the family we want?

Name of family member	How each can use talents and skills to help build the family we want

3. On the Operational Task List on pages 141-145, determine which family member owns each activity, paying special attention to the ones that received yellow and red dots.

continued

week 4

Activity 9
Contributions (continued)

4. On the Family ROI Journey Map section #9 marked *Contributions*, write each family member's key contributions.

5. Discuss your top three "hot spots"—the most critical tasks with room for improvement—and complete an action plan on page 146 for each. Keep things simple and manageable by picking just a few things that have the biggest impact. Consider the following:

    a. What is the problem?

    b. Why is this happening?

    c. How can we fix it?

    d. Who will own it?

    e. When will it be completed?

See It in Action

The Rivera family has found that since each member brings unique talents to the family, it's helpful to designate specific roles explicitly. "That way," Lesli explains, "everyone knows who is doing what. And there is no right or wrong—it's whatever works best for your family. In our family, Stan has the talent for cooking so he handles the meals. It's an arrangement that our kids have grown up with. Once we were watching a TV show where the mom was making dinner. Lauren, who was three at the time, and used to seeing her dad cook dinner every night, gasped in surprise and said, 'I didn't know mommies can cook!'"

WHAT   WHO   HOW OFTEN?
(e.g., once a year, monthly, weekly, daily)

WHAT	WHO	HOW OFTEN?
Family & Social Activities		
Plan family outings		
Plan social events (birthday parties, dinner parties)		
Plan vacations		
Call relatives and friends		
Make gifts/cards		
Take pictures		
Create photo albums/slide shows		
Schedule date nights		
Send cards (thank you, birthday, holidays)		
Other		
Outdoor Maintenance		
Maintain yard (mow lawn, rake leaves, shovel snow)		
Maintain garden (pull weeds, plant vegetables)		
Manage major outdoor projects (landscaping, building play structures, putting up fences)		
Maintain and repair car(s)		
Wash car(s)		
Manage home improvements (carpentry, painting, roofing)		

week 4

continued

WHAT	WHO	HOW OFTEN?
Clean gutters		
Other		
Shopping and Errands		
Buy groceries		
Run errands		
Buy household supplies		
Buy clothing and shoes		
Make large purchases (car, TV)		
Buy gifts		
Take items to dry cleaner		
Other		
Scheduling		
Maintain family calendar/schedule		
Coordinate family and work hours		
Plan family meetings		
Schedule appointments at home (repair services, housecleaners, deliveries) and be available		
Schedule classes, workshops, after-school activities		
Other		
Finances		
Plan budget and debt management		
Pay bills		
Prepare taxes		

WHAT	WHO	HOW OFTEN?
Manage retirement planning		
Manage savings and plan for large purchases (car, education)		
Manage insurance, wills, living trusts		
Other		
Indoor Maintenance		
Straighten up the house, put things away		
Clean the house (dust, vacuum, sweep, clean bathrooms)		
Take out garbage		
Wash laundry		
Prepare for guests		
Decorate house (regular ongoing projects)		
Decorate for holidays or special occasions		
Do small repairs around the house		
Manage computers and technology (purchase, maintenance)		
Organize and restock emergency kit (fire, earthquake, tornado, hurricane, tsunami)		

continued

week 4

WHAT	WHO	HOW OFTEN?
Plan and practice emergency and safety procedures (fire, earthquake, tornado, tsunami)		
Manage organizational projects (clean closets, garage)		
Other		
Food Preparation and Cleanup		
Plan meals		
Make breakfast		
Make or pack school lunches		
Cook dinner		
Wash dishes		
Baking, canning or other special food projects		
Other		
Wellness		
Schedule doctor, dentist, and other wellness care		
Create exercise routine		
Lead/organize spiritual practices		
Plan stress management activities		
Participate in hobbies and personal enrichment		
Schedule personal grooming (e.g. haircuts)		
Other		

WHAT	WHO	HOW OFTEN?
Pet Care		
Feed pet(s)		
Play with pet(s) and/or take pet(s) for walk		
Take pet(s) to vet		
Other		
Child and Elder Care		
Feed		
Bathe		
Change/dress		
Transport to doctor, dentist, or orthodontist		
Transport to activities		
Play and read to/with		
Manage morning routine		
Manage evening routine		
Get up at night		
Plan and attend activities		
Coordinate, participate in school activities (PTA, volunteer in classroom, sports coach, club advisor, college visits)		
Help with homework		
Help learn new skills		
Manage behavior and discipline		
Other		

week 4

Family Action Plan

		ACTION	WHO	BY WHEN
Hot Spot 1		1		
		2		
		3		
Hot Spot 2		1		
		2		
		3		
Hot Spot 3		1		
		2		
		3		

Sample of Family Action Plan

		ACTION	WHO	BY WHEN
1 Hot Spot	Family Health – start eating more healthful foods	1 Agree on weekly menu	Family / Mom	Every Sunday
		2 Create a weekly shopping list	Mom	Every Sunday
		3 Make lunches the night before	Dad	Nightly Sun–Thurs

Just for Kids: How Can I Help

Children can identify ways they can help out in the family.

- In advance, download the Family ROI Age-Appropriate Chores List from www.familyroi.org.

- Create the How Can I Help game by cutting copies of the Age Appropriate Chores list into strips, with one chore listed on each strip. Make one set for each child.

- Ask each child what they think they are good at.

- Discuss how they can use their skills to help out at home.

- Provide the kids with the How Can I Help card game.

- Have kids sort the chores into age groups, trying to guess the earliest age they think kids can do them.

- Have each kid pick one activity that they will start to do at home to help.

- Write it on a piece of paper and insert the paper into their scrapbook.

"I don't care how poor a man is; if he has family, he's rich."

—Dan Wilcox and Thad Mumford, "Identity Crisis," *M*A*S*H*

Week 4

APPRECIATION

Congratulations! You've accomplished a lot with your family during the Family ROI Experience. Together, you've practiced ways to communicate compassionately with one another, designed your family's culture, painted a picture of your future, and looked at the processes that will keep your family running smoothly.

We're now on the final and very important step of our journey: Appreciation.

Feeling valued is a deep human need. Recognizing and expressing gratitude brings people closer together. Nowhere is it more important to notice and express appreciation for each other than at home. We love the way author Sara Paddison puts it in her book *The Hidden Power of the Heart*: "Appreciating each other is a true family value, one that will bail out much of the stress on the planet and help strengthen the universal bond all people have."

Sometimes a simple "thank you" is all that is needed to let someone know we appreciate them. However, to ensure that we most effectively express our appreciation, we can go beyond "thank you" and use compassionate communication strategies by conveying the following:

1. This is what you did.
2. This is how I feel.
3. These are my needs that were met.

Here is a good example of expressing appreciation without Compassionate Communication:

GOOD: "Caitlin, you're such a good girl! Thanks for being so quiet!"

Here is an even better example of expressing appreciation by using Compassionate Communication:

BETTER: "Caitlin, thank you for playing so quietly while the baby was napping. I felt very calm and happy. I need everyone to be well-rested so we can enjoy the party later."

Steps	What to say
1. This is what you did.	Thank you for playing so quietly while the baby was napping.
2. This is how I feel.	I felt very calm and happy.
3. These are my needs that were met.	I need everyone to be well-rested so we can enjoy the party later.

How deeply do we need to feel valued as individuals? To answer, here is a true story that appeared in the magazine *Reader's Digest*.[25] It's about a junior high school teacher who had a student named Mark who was bright and sometimes mischievous. Mark was charming and polite, but he also talked a lot and made other students laugh during class.

One day, things just didn't feel right to the teacher. She could tell that the students were worn out by their schoolwork. They were

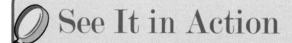

See It in Action

For Angie and Nate Lackey, the Family ROI appreciation exercise had a lasting effect. Today, the family wraps appreciation into their family huddles and everyday life. "Who doesn't enjoy hearing good things about themselves? It goes a long way," Angie reflected. "We always try to end (our meetings) with that."

When two of the Lackey kids aren't getting along, Angie and Nate put them on the same team doing household chores together. "Then we have them tell each other what they like about each other. We'll say, 'I understand this really upset you, but also tell us something great about your sister.' One of them might say, 'Well, she's got a very caring heart.'" Expressing appreciation has also made a difference in their marriage. In any partnership, there are times when you don't appreciate the other person and you only see the negative. To remedy this, Angie says, "It's just taking a minute to stop and say, 'I really appreciate when you pick up your clothes. That means a lot to me.'"

week

4

See It in Action

Tauha Te Kani and his wife Gayle from Gisborne, New Zealand, had already been married for 12 years when they learned from Family ROI about consciously weaving appreciation into their lives. One morning, Gayle told Tauha that she sees him as strong and dependable and as reliable as a big Acacia tree. "Over the years of our marriage," she told him, "you have developed into a beautiful wood that can be used to make fine things, like beautiful furniture and treasure chests. You reach out your branches and touch people in the community and in our lives," she added. Tauha's still talking about what his wife told him that morning. "I was like, 'Wow!'" Tauha said. "That was just…I was just blown away! It was a great way to start the day!"

getting frustrated with themselves and edgy with one another. So, she decided to try something different. She asked the students to write the names of all their classmates on two sheets of paper, leaving a space between each name. Then she told them to think of the nicest thing they could say about each of their classmates and write it down.

That weekend, the teacher wrote down the name of each student on fresh sheets of paper, one for each student. She listed everything their classmates had said about them. On Monday, she gave each student his or her list and watched them smile. One student whispered, "Really?" Another said quietly, "I never knew the others liked me so much." Still another said, "I can't believe it." The mood in the classroom was completely transformed.

Many years passed and no one ever mentioned the papers again. The teacher wasn't sure if the students shared them with each other or with their parents. But then, one day, she learned that one of her former students had been killed in Vietnam. It was Mark, and his parents wanted to know if she could attend his funeral. The church was packed with Mark's friends. It was a rainy day, which made it even sadder. Mark's coffin was draped in an American flag.

After the funeral, Mark's mother and father approached the teacher and said, "We want to show you something." Mark's father reached in his pocket and said, "They found this on Mark when he was killed. We thought you might recognize it." Mark's dad carefully removed two worn pieces of notebook paper that had been taped, folded, and refolded many times. The teacher recognized it as being one of the lists she had given her students, this one with all the good things they had said about Mark. "Thank you for doing that," Mark's mother said. "As you can see, he treasured it."

Later that day, some of Mark's classmates told the teacher how they, too, had saved their lists. One kept it in her diary, another in her purse. "I think we all kept our lists," one student told her. That's when the teacher finally sat down and cried.

Who can better appreciate us than our families? But, if we don't share our feelings with our loved ones, they'll never know. So, why not start now? ■

Just for Kids: Appreciation Activity

Children can reflect on what they appreciate most about their family members.

- Help each child create an appreciation card for each member of their family, including siblings. Have each child write or dictate (depending on age) what he or she appreciates about each family member.

- Kids can decorate the cards when they are finished.

- Insert the papers into their scrapbook when they are complete.

week

4

Activity 10
Appreciation

1. Move your game piece to #10 *Appreciation* on the Family ROI Journey Map.

2. Take one piece of paper for each of your family members.

3. Write one name at the top of each paper.

4. Distribute one paper to each person.

5. Spend a few minutes writing down what you appreciate most about the family member listed at the top of the page.

6. Pass the sheets around so everyone has a chance to write about each family member.

7. When everyone is finished, each family member should be given all the sheets of paper with his or her name at the top.

8. Take a moment to read what your family members appreciate about you.

9. In the Family ROI Journey Map section #10 marked *Appreciation*, write each family member's name with a brief summary of what the family most appreciates about him or her.

ENJOY!

Your Best Family Today and Tomorrow

Years ago, Stan and Lesli went on a cycling vacation, pedaling through the Canadian Rockies. Along with 17 other cyclists, they found themselves traversing Alberta's Icefields Parkway from Banff to Jasper. As they rode, they were rewarded with countless wildlife sightings, views of dramatic glaciers, and stops at turquoise lakes and pounding waterfalls. Yet those same beautiful Rockies also inspired some anxiety about what they knew lay ahead—100 miles up a steep mountain grade through the Sunwapta Pass.

At breakfast, their guide prepared them. It would be a difficult climb, he warned, with an altitude gain of 2,000 feet. Before setting off, each rider needed to decide whether to bike the entire distance or ride part of the way in the support van that ferried their gear from campsite to campsite.

> "I didn't come all this way to ride in the van."

The van sounded like a tempting offer. One hundred miles up a mountain seemed overwhelming, especially since they had already been riding for four days straight.

All of the cyclists nervously questioned each other before making a commitment: "Are you going to try it? I don't know.… What do you think?"

"Brantley, what are you going to do?" Lesli asked a man who was thirty years her senior. Brantley, who was from North Carolina, looked at her slowly and deliberately before he said, "Lesli, I didn't come all this way to ride in the van."

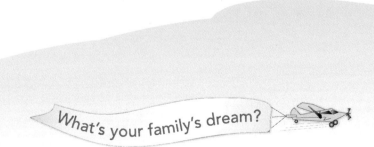

What's your family's dream?

That did it. Brantley was right. Stan and Lesli had lost sight of the fact that they hadn't come to ride in the van either. So they didn't. And they made it up the mountain on their own peddle power.

Ever since, the phrase "I didn't come all this way to ride in the van" has been a mantra for Lesli and Stan, especially whenever they find themselves feeling afraid or hesitant to chase a long-held dream, or when their family starts drifting in a different direction from where they want to go. Lesli said, "It's much too easy to lose sight of what we originally set out to do—of what our true desires are—and instead allow life to pass in a blur, to just make it to Friday, or to just 'ride in the van.'"

That's why we created Family ROI, and why our families put the Family ROI tools to use on a regular basis. We've found it's not enough to create a vision, set goals, and forget about them. As our lives change, our goals and needs do, too. The Family ROI Experience can be used over and over again to stay on course, change course, and make your dreams come true.

Which brings us to a question: What's your family's dream?

Here at Family ROI, we hope you won't let the years pass in a blur, accumulating wistful regrets from time spent "riding in the van." Instead, we hope you can create your very best family and achieve all that you desire. When you do, please let us know. We'd love to hear all about it! ■

NOTES

1. Retrouvaille. http://www.retrouvaille.org

2. Rebecca J. North, et al., "Family Support, Family Income, and Happiness: A 10-Year Perspective," *Journal of Family Psychology* 22 (3) (2008): 475-483.

3. Child Trends. "The Family Environment and Adolescent Well-Being: Exposure to Positive and Negative Family Influences." http://www.childtrends.org/Files/FamilyEnvironmentRB.pdf.

4. The Office of Juvenile Justice and Delinquency Prevention (OJJDP). "Family Skills Training for Parents and Children." http://www.ncjrs.gov/pdffiles1/ojjdp/180140.pdf.

5. Celebrate Green. "Family Traditions: The 'Glue' That Holds Families Together." http://www.celebrategreen.net/blog/everyday-celebrations/family-traditions-the-glue-that-holds-families-together.

6. Barbara H. Fiese, et al., "Family Rituals in the Early Stages of Parenthood," *Journal of Marriage and the Family* 55 (3) (1993): 633-642.

7. Michael P. Farrell, Grace M. Barnes, and Sarbani Banerjee, "Family Cohesion as a Buffer Against the Effects of Problem-Drinking Fathers on Psychological Distress, Deviant Behavior, and Heavy Drinking in Adolescents," *Journal of Health and Social Behavior* 36 (1995): 377-385.

8. Elizabeth Agnvall, "Bundles of . . . Misery. Parenting Got You Down? You're Not Alone, Says Study." *The Washington Post*, January 3, 2006. http://www.washingtonpost.com/wp-dyn/content/article/2006/01/02/AR2006010201513.html.

9. Puppets can be ordered at www.familyroi.org.

10. Marshall Rosenberg, *Nonviolent Communication: A Language of Life*. (California: PuddleDancer Press, 2003).

11. Meg Cox, *The Book of New Family Traditions*. (Pennsylvania: Running Press, 2003). Reprinted by permission of the publisher.

12. Family ROI Talking Stick craft kits can be ordered at www.familyroi.org.

13. John P. Kotter and James L. Heskett, *Corporate Culture and Performance*. (New York: The Free Press, 1992).

14. Scott A. Christofferson, Robert S. McNish, and Diane L. Sias, "Where Mergers Go Wrong," *McKinsey Quarterly* (2004).

15. Wharton University. "Why Do So Many Mergers Fail?" http://www.wharton.universia.net/index.cfm?fa=viewArticle&id=927&language=english.

16. Family ROI Values card decks can be ordered at www.familyroi.org.

17. Deborah Lupton, *Food, the Body, and the Self*. (California: Sage Publications, 1996).

18. Meg Cox, *The Book of New Family Traditions*. (Pennsylvania: Running Press, 2003). Reprinted by permission of the publisher.

19. The National Center on Addiction and Substance Abuse (CASA) at Columbia University. "The Importance of Family Dinners." http://www.casacolumbia.org/templates/publications_reports.aspx.

20. Interbrand. "Best Global Brands 2009 Rankings." http://www.interbrand.com/best_global_brands.aspx.

21. Salary.com. "Salary.com's 10th Annual Mom Salary Survey Reveals Stay-at-Home Moms Would Earn US$117,856." http://press.salary.com/easyir/customrel.do?easyirid=C62ED049D69BA1E0&version=live&prid=615803&releasejsp=custom_117.

22. John O'Neil, "Behavior: How Rituals Enhance Well-Being," *New York Times*, December 10, 2002, http://www.nytimes.com/2002/12/10/health/vital-signs-behavior-how-rituals-enhance-well-being.html.

23. eHow. "Top Things Couples Argue About." http://www.ehow.com/list_6472771_top-things-couples-argue.html.

24. Catherine Rampell, "Money Fights Predict Divorce Rates," *New York Times*, December 7, 2009, http://economix.blogs.nytimes.com/2009/12/07/money-fights-predict-divorce-rates/.

25. Sister Helen P. Mrosla, "Good Night Sister. Thank you for Teaching Me!", *Reader's Digest*, October 1991; based on the original article, "Good Night Sister. Thank You for Teaching Me!" in *Proteus: A Journal of Ideas*, Spring 1991. Reprinted by permission of the publisher.

Made in the USA
Middletown, DE
13 September 2021